# Esoteric Buddhism

A.P. Sinnett

President of the London Lodge
of the Theosophical Society

First published 2012
Copyright © 2012 Aziloth Books

All Rights Reserved. No part of this publication may be reproduced, stored in a retrieval system or transmitted in any form or by any means, electronic, mechanical, photocopying, recording, scanning or otherwise, except under the terms of the Copyright Licensing Agency Ltd, 90 Tottenham Court Road, London, W1P 0LP, UK, without the permission in writing of the Publisher. Requests to the Publisher should be via email to: info@azilothbooks.com.

Every effort has been made to contact all copyright holders. The publisher will be glad to make good in future editions any errors or omissions brought to their attention.

This publication is designed to provide authoritative and accurate information in regard to the subject matter covered. It is sold on the understanding that the Publisher is not engaged in rendering professional services.

British Library Cataloguing in Publication Data

A catalogue record for this book is available from the British Library

ISBN-13: 978-1-908388-74-2

Printed and bound in Great Britain by Lightning Souce UK Ltd., 6 Precedent Drive, Rooksley, Milton Keynes MK13 8PR.

Cover Illustration: *The Fasting Buddha.* Unknown Artist.
Gandharan Art - Kushana Period.
(c. 2nd century B.C.–3rd century A.D)

Fifth edition.

Annotated and enlarged by the author

# CONTENTS

Preface to the Annotated Edition — 6

Preface to the Original Edition — 11

**CHAPTER I Esoteric Teachers** — 15
Nature of the Present Exposition - Seclusion of Eastern Knowledge - The Arhats and their Attributes - The Mahatmas - Occultists generally - Isolated Mystics - Inferior Yogis - Occult Training - The Great Purpose -Its Incidental Consequences - Present Concessions

**CHAPTER II The Constitution of Man** — 25
Esoteric Cosmogony - Where to Begin - Working back from Man to Universe - Analysis of Man - The Seven Principles

**CHAPTER III The Planetary Chain** — 33
Esoteric Views of Evolution - The Chain of Globes - Progress of Man round them - The Spiral Advance - Original Evolution of the Globes - The Lower Kingdoms

**CHAPTER IV The World Periods** — 42
Uniformity of Nature- Rounds and Races - The Septenary Law - Objective and Subjective Lives - Total Incarnations - Former Races on Earth - Periodic Cataclysms - Atlantis - Lemuria - The Cyclic Law

**CHAPTER V Devachan** — 53
Spiritual Destinies of the Ego - Karma - Division of the Principles of Death - Progress of the Higher Duad - Existence in Devachan - Subjective Progress - Avitchi - Earthly Connection with Devachan - Devachanic Periods

**CHAPTER VI Kâma loca** — 65
The Astral Shell - Its Habitat - Its Nature - Surviving Impulses - Elementals - Mediums and Shells - Accidents and Suicides - Lost Personalities

CHAPTER VII The Human Tide-Wave ......... 81
Progress of the Main Wave - Obscurations - Twilight and
Dawn of Evolution - Our Neighbouring Planets - Gradations
of Spirituality - Prematurely Developed Egos - Intervals of
Re-Incarnation

CHAPTER VIII The Progress of Humanity ......... 90
The Choice of Good or Evil - The Second Half of Evolution
- The Decisive Turning-point - Spirituality and Intellect -
The Survival of the Fittest - The Sixth Sense - Development of the
Principles in their Order - The Subsidence of the Unfit - Provision
for All - The Exceptional Cases - Their Scientific Explanation - Justice
Satisfied - The Destiny of Failures - Human Evolution Reviewed

CHAPTER IX Buddha ......... 100
The Esoteric Buddha - Re-Incarnations of Adepts - Buddha's
Incarnation - The Seven Buddhas of the Great Races - Avalokiteshwara -
Addi Buddha - Adeptship in Buddha's Time - Sankaracharya - Vedantin
Doctrines - Tsong-kapa - Occult Reforms in Tibet

CHAPTER X  Nirvana Its Remoteness ......... 110
- Preceding Gradations - Partial Nirvana - The Threshold of Nirvana -
Nirvana - Para Nirvana - Buddha and Nirvana - Nirvana attained
by Adepts - General Progress towards Nirvana - Conditions of its
Attainment - Spirituality and Religion - The Pursuit of Truth

CHAPTER XI The Universe ......... 115
The Days and Night of Brahma - The Various Manvantaras and Pralayas
- The Solar System - The Universal Pralaya - Recommencement of
Evolution - "Creation" - The Great First Cause - The Eternal Cyclic Process

CHAPTER XII The Doctrine Reviewed ......... 122
Correspondences of the Esoteric Doctrine with Visible Nature - Free
Will and Predestination - The Origin of Evil - Geology, Biology, and
the Esoteric Teaching - Buddhism and Scholarship - The Origins of
all Things - The Doctrine as Distorted - The Ultimate Dissolutions
of Consciousness - Transmigration - The Soul and the Spirit -
Personality and Individuality - Karma

Bibliography ......... 137

## PREFACE TO THE ANNOTATED EDITION

Since this book was first published in the beginning of 1883, I have come into possession of much additional information bearing on many of the problems dealt with. But I am glad to say that such later teaching only reveals incompleteness in my original conception of the esoteric doctrine, - no material error so far. Indeed I have received from the great Adept himself, from whom I obtained my instruction in the first instance, the assurance that the book as it now stands is a sound and trustworthy statement of the scheme of Nature as understood by the initiates of occult science, which may have to be a good deal developed in the future, if the interest it excites is keen enough to constitute an efficient demand for further teaching of this kind on the part of the world at large, but will never have to be remodelled or apologized for. In view of this assurance it seems best that I should now put forward my later conclusions and additional information in the form of annotations on each branch of the subject, rather than infuse them into the original text, which, under the circumstances, I am reluctant in any way to alter. I have therefore adopted that plan in the present edition.

As conveying an indirect acknowledgement of the general harmony to be traced between these teachings and the recognized philosophical tenets of certain other great schools of Indian thought, I may here refer to criticisms on this book, which were published in the Indian magazine the Theosophist in June, 1883, by "a Brahman Hindoo." The writer complains that in interpreting the esoteric doctrine, I have departed unnecessarily from accepted Sanskrit nomenclature; but his objection merely is that I have given unfamiliar names in some cases to ideas already embodied in Hindoo sacred writings, and that I have done too much honour to the religious system commonly known as Buddhism, by representing that as more closely allied with the esoteric doctrine than any other. "The popular wisdom of the majority of Hindoos to this day," says my Brahman critic, "is more or less tinged with the esoteric doctrine taught in Mr Sinnett's book misnamed 'Esoteric Buddhism," while there is not a single village or hamlet in the whole of India in which people are not more or less acquainted with the sublime tenets of the Vedanta philosophy . . . . The effects of Karma in the next birth, the enjoyment of its fruits, good or evil, in a subjective or spiritual state of existence prior to the reincarnation of the spiritual monad in this or any other world, the loitering of the unsatisfied souls or human shells in the earth (Kama loca), the pralayic and manvantaric periods . . . . are not only intelligible, but are even familiar to a great many Hindoos, under names different from those made use by the author of 'Esoteric Buddhism.' " So much the better", - I take leave to rejoin, - from the point of view of Western readers, to whom it must be a matter of indifference whether the esoteric Hindoo or Buddhist religion is nearest to absolutely true spiritual science, which should certainly bear no name that appears to wed it to any one faith in the external world more than to another. All that we in Europe can be anxious for, is to arrive at a clear understanding as to the essential principles of that science, and if we find the principles defined in this book claimed by the cultured representatives of more than one great Oriental creed as equally the underlying truths of their different systems, we shall be all the better inclined to believe the present exposition of doctrine worth our attention.

In regard to the complaint itself, that the teachings here reduced to an intelligible shape are incorrectly described by the name this book bears, I cannot do better than quote the note by which the editor of the Theosophist replies to his Brahman contributor. This note says: -"We print the above letter as it expresses in courteous language, and in an able manner, the views of a large number of our Hindoo brothers. At the same time it must be stated that the name of 'Esoteric Buddhism' was given to Mr Sinnett's latest publication, not because the doctrine propounded therein is meant to be specially identified with any particular form of faith, but because Buddhism means the doctrine of the Buddhas, the Wise i.e. the Wisdom Religion." For my own part I need only add that I fully accept and adopt that explanation of the matter. It would indeed be a misconception of the design which this book is intended to sub-serve, to suppose it concerned with the recommendation, to a dilettante modern taste, of Old World fashions in religious thought. The external forms and fancies of religion in one age may be a little purer, in another a little more corrupt, but they inevitably adapt themselves to their period, and it would be extravagant to imagine them interchangeable. The present statement is not put forward in the hope of making Buddhists from among the adherents of any other system, but with the view of conveying to thoughtful readers, as well in the East as in the West, a series of leading ideas relating to the actual verities of Nature, and the real facts of man's progress through evolution, which have been communicated to the present writer by Eastern philosophers, and thus fall most readily into an Oriental mould. For the value of these teachings will perhaps be most fully realized when we clearly perceive that they are scientific in their character rather than controversial. Spiritual truths, if they are truths, may evidently be dealt with in a no less scientific spirit than chemical reactions. And no religious feeling, of whatever colour it may be, need be disturbed by the importation into the general stock of knowledge of new discoveries about the constitution and nature of man on the plane of his higher activities. True religion will eventually find a way to assimilate much fresh knowledge, in the same way that it always finally acquiesces in a general enlargement of Knowledge on the physical plane. This, in the first instance, may sometimes disconcert notions associated with religious belief, - as geological science at first embarrassed biblical chronology. But in time men came to see that the essence of the biblical statement does not reside in the literal sense of the cosmological passages in the Old Testament, and religious conceptions grew all the purer for the relief thus afforded. In just the same way when positive scientific knowledge begins to embrace a comprehension of the laws relating to the spiritual development of man, -some misconceptions of Nature, long blended with religion, may have to give way, but still it will be found that the central ideas of true religion have been cleared up and strengthened all the better for the process. Especially as such processes continue, will the internal dissensions of the religious world be inevitably subdued. The warfare of sects can only be due to a failure on the part of rival sectarians to grasp fundamental facts. Could a time come when the basic ideas on which religion rests, should be comprehended with the same certainty with which we comprehend some primary physical laws, and disagreement about them be recognized by all educated people as ridiculous, then there would not be room for very acrimonious divergences of religious sentiment. Externals of religious thought would still differ in different climates and among different races, - as dress and dietaries differ, - but such differences would not give rise to intellectual antagonism.

Basic facts of the nature indicated are developed, it appears to me, in the exposition of spiritual science we have now obtained from our Eastern friends. It is quite unnecessary for religious thinkers to turn aside from them under the impression that they are arguments in favour of some Eastern, in preference to the more general Western creed. If medical science were to discover a new fact about man's body, were to unveil some hitherto concealed principle on which the growth of skin and flesh and bone is carried on, that discovery would not be regarded as trenching at all on the domain of religion. Would the domain of religion be invaded, for example, by a discovery that should go one step behind the action of the nerves, and disclose a finer set of activities manipulating these as they manipulate the muscles? At all events, even if such a discovery might begin to reconcile science and religion, no man who allows any of his higher faculties to enter into his religious thinking would put aside a positive fact of Nature, plainly shown to be such, as hostile to religion. Being a fact it would inevitably fit in with all other facts, and with religious truth among the number. So with the great mass of information in reference to the spiritual evolution of man embodied in the present statement. Our best plan evidently is to ask, before we look into the report I bring forward, not whether it will square in all respects with preconceived views, but whether it really does introduce us to a series of natural facts connected with the growth and development of man's higher faculties. If it does this we may wisely examine the facts first in the scientific spirit, and leave them to exercise whatever effect on collateral belief may be reasonable and legitimate later on.

Ramifying, as the explanation proceeds, into a great many side paths, it will be seen that the central statement now put forward constitutes a theory of anthropology which completes and spiritualises the ordinary notions of physical evolution. The theory which traces man's development by successive and very gradual improvements of animal forms from generation to generation, is a very barren and miserable theory regarded as an all-embracing account of creation; but properly understood it paves the way for a comprehension of the higher concurrent process which is all the while evolving the soul of man in the spiritual realm of existence. The present view of the matter reconciles the evolutionary method with the deeply seated craving of every self-conscious entity for perpetuity of individual life. The disjointed series of improving forms on this earth have no individuality, and the life of each in turn is a separate transaction which finds in the next similar transaction, no compensation for suffering involved, no justice, no fruit of its efforts. It is just possible to argue on the assumption of a new independent creation of a human soul every time a new human form is produced by physiological growth, that in the after spiritual states of such soul, justice may be awarded; but then this conception is itself at variance with the fundamental idea of evolution, which traces, or believes that it traces the origin of each soul to the workings of highly developed matter in each case. Nor is it less at variance with the analogies of Nature; but without going into that, it is enough for the moment to perceive that the theory of spiritual evolution, as set forth in the teaching of esoteric science, is at any rate in harmony with these analogies, while at the same time it satisfactorily meets the requirements of justice, and of the instinctive demand for continuity of individual life.

This theory recognizes the evolution of the soul as a process that is quite continuous in itself, though carried out partly through the instrumentality of a great series of dissociated forms. Putting aside for the moment of profound metaphysics of the theory which trace the principle of life from the original first cause of the cosmos, we find the soul as an entity emerging from the animal kingdom, and passing into the earliest human forms, without being at that time ripe for the higher intellectual life with which the present state of humanity renders us familiar. But through successive incarnations in forms whose physical improvement, under the Darwinian law, is constantly fitting them to be its habitation at each return to objective life, it gradually gathers that enormous range of experience which is summed up in its higher development. In the intervals between its physical incarnations it prolongs and works out, and finally exhausts or transmutes into so much abstract development, the personal experiences of each life. This is the clue to the true explanation of that apparent difficulty which besets the cruder form of the theory of reincarnation which independent speculation has sometimes thrown out.

Each man is unconscious of having led previous lives, therefore he contends that subsequent lives can afford him no compensation for this one. He overlooks the enormous importance of the intervening spiritual condition, in which he by no means forgets the personal adventures and emotions he has just passed through, and in the course of which he distills these into so much cosmic progress. In the following pages the elucidation of this profoundly interesting mystery is attempted, and it will be seen that the view of events now afforded us is not only a solution of the problems of life and death, but of many very perplexing experiences on the borderland between those conditions - or rather between physical and spiritual life - which have engaged attention and speculation so widely of recent years in most civilized countries.

# PREFACE TO THE ORIGINAL EDITION

The teachings embodied in the present volume let in a flood of light on questions connected with Buddhist doctrine which have deeply perplexed previous writers on the religion, and offer the world for the first time a practical clue to the meaning of almost all ancient religious symbolism. More than this, the esoteric doctrine, when properly understood, will be found to advance an overpowering claim on the attention of earnest thinkers. Its tenets are not presented to us as the invention of any founder or prophet. Its testimony is based on no written scriptures. Its views of Nature have been evolved by the researches of an immense succession of investigators, qualified for their task by the possession of spiritual faculties and perceptions of a higher order than those belonging to ordinary humanity. In the course of ages the block of knowledge thus accumulated, concerning the origin of the world and of man and the ultimate destinies of our race - concerning also the nature of other worlds and states of existence differing from those of our present life - checked and examined at every point, verified in all directions, and constantly under examination throughout, has come to be looked on by its custodians as constituting the absolute truth concerning spiritual things, the actual state of the facts regarding vast regions of vital activity lying beyond this earthly existence.

European philosophy, whether concerned with religion or pure metaphysics, has so long been used to a sense of insecurity in speculations outrunning the limits of physical experiment, that absolute truth about spiritual things is hardly recognized any longer by prudent thinkers as a reasonable object of pursuit; but different habits of thought have been acquired in Asia. The secret doctrine which, to a considerable extent, I am now enabled to expound, is regarded not only by all its adherents, but by vast numbers who have never expected to know more of it than that such a doctrine exists, as a mine of entirely trustworthy knowledge from which all religions and philosophies have derived whatever they possess of truth, and with which every religion must coincide if it claims to be a mode of expression for truth.

This is a bold claim, but I venture to announce the following exposition as one of immense importance to the world, because I believe that claim can be substantiated.

I do not say that within the compass of this volume the authenticity of the esoteric doctrine can be proved. Such proof cannot be given by any process of argument; only through the development in each inquirer for himself of the faculties required for the direct observation of Nature along the lines indicated. But his prima facie conclusion may be determined by the extent to which the views of Nature about to be unfolded, may recommend themselves to his mind, and by the reasons which exist for trusting the powers of observation of those by whom they are communicated.

Will it be supposed that the very magnitude of the claim now made on behalf of the esoteric doctrine, lifts the present statement out of the region of inquiry to which its title refers - inquiry as to the real inner meaning of the definite and specific religion called Buddhism? The fact is, however, that esoteric Buddhism, though by no means divorced from the associations of exoteric Buddhism, must not be conceived to constitute a mere imperium in imperio - a central school of culture in the vortex of the Buddhist world. In proportion as Buddhism retreats into the inner penetralia of its faith, these are found to merge into the inner penetralia of other faiths. The cosmic conceptions, and the knowledge of Nature on which Buddhism not merely rests, but which constitute esoteric Buddhism, equally constitute esoteric Brahmanism. And the esoteric doctrine is thus regarded by those of all creeds who are "enlightened" (in the Buddhist sense) as the absolute truth concerning Nature, Man, the origin of the Universe, and the destinies toward which its inhabitants are tending. At the same time, exoteric Buddhism has remained in closer union with the esoteric doctrine than any other popular religion. An exposition of the inner knowledge, addressed to English readers in the present day, will thus associate itself irresistibly with familiar outlines of Buddhist teaching. It will certainly impart to these a living meaning they generally seem to be without, but all the more on this account may the esoteric doctrine be most conveniently studied in its Buddhist aspect: one, moreover, which has been so strongly impressed upon it since the time of Gautama Buddha that though the essence of the doctrine dates back to a far more remote antiquity, the Buddhist colouring has now permeated its whole substance. That which I am about to put before the reader is esoteric Buddhism, and for European students approaching it for the first time, any other designation would be a misnomer.

The statement I have to make must be considered in its entirety before the reader will be able to comprehend why initiates in the esoteric doctrine regard the concession involved in the present disclosures of the general outlines of this doctrine as one of startling magnitude. One explanation of this feeling, however, may be readily seen to spring from the extreme sacredness that has always been attached by their ancient guardians to the inner vital truths of Nature. Hitherto this sacredness has always prescribed their absolute concealment from the profane herd. And so far as that policy of concealment, - the tradition of countless ages, - is now being given up, the new departure which the appearance of this volume signalizes will be contemplated with surprise and regret by a great many initiated disciples. The surrender to criticism which may sometimes perhaps be clumsy and irreverent, of doctrines which have hitherto been regarded by such persons as too majestic in their import to be talked of at all except under circumstances of befitting solemnity, will seem to them a terrible profanation of the great mysteries. From the European point of view it would be unreasonable to expect that such a book as this can be exempt from the usual rough-and-tumble treatment of new ideas. And special convictions or common-place bigotry may sometimes render such treatment in the present case peculiarly inimical. But all that, though a matter of course to European exponents of the doctrine like myself, will seem very grievous and disgusting to its earlier and more regular representatives. They will appeal sadly to the wisdom of the time-honoured rule which, in the old symbolical way, forbade the initiates from casting pearls before swine.

Happily, as I think, the rule has not been allowed to operate any longer to the prejudice of those who, while still far from being initiated, in the occult sense of the term, will probably have become, by sheer force of modern culture, qualified to appreciate the concession.

Part of the information contained in the following pages was first thrown out in a fragmentary form in the Theosophist, a monthly magazine, published at Madras, by the leaders of the Theosophical Society. As almost all the articles referred to have been my own writing, I have not hesitated to weld parts of them, when this course has been convenient, into the present volume. A certain advantage is gained by thus showing how the separate pieces of the mosaic as first presented to public notice, drop naturally into their places in the (comparatively) finished pavement.

The doctrine or system now disclosed in its broad outlines has been so jealously guarded hitherto, that no mere literary researches, though they might have curry-combed all India, could have brought to light any morsel of the information thus revealed. It is given out to the world at last by the free grace of those in whose keeping it has hitherto lain. Nothing could ever have extorted from them its very first letter. It is only after a perusal of the present explanations that their position generally, as regards their present disclosures or their previous reticence can be criticized or even comprehended. The views of Nature now put forward are altogether unfamiliar to European thinkers; the policy of the graduates in esoteric knowledge, which has grown out of their long intimacy with these views must be considered in connection with the peculiar bearings of the doctrine itself.

As for the circumstances under which these revelations were first foreshadowed in the Theosophist, and are now rounded off and expanded as my readers will perceive, it is enough for the moment to say, that the Theosophical Society, through my connection with which the materials dealt with in this volume have come into my hands, owes its establishment to certain persons who are among the custodians of esoteric science. The information poured out at last for the benefit of all who are ripe to receive it, has been destined for communication to the world through the Theosophical Society since the foundation of that body, and later circumstances only have indicated myself as the agent through whom the communication could be conveniently made.

Let me add, that I do not regard myself as the sole exponent for the outer world, at this crisis, of esoteric truth. These teachings are the outcome, as regards philosophical knowledge, of the relations with the outer world which have been established by the custodians of esoteric truth through me. And it is only regarding the acts and intentions of those esoteric teachers who have chosen to work through me, that I can have any certain knowledge. But, in different ways, some other writers seem to be engaged in expounding for the benefit of the world - and, as I believe, in accordance with a great plan, of which this volume is a part - the same truths, in different aspects, that I am commissioned to unfold. Probably the great activity at present of literary speculation dealing with problems that overstep the range of physical knowledge, may also be in some way provoked by that policy, on the part of the great custodians of esoteric truth, of which my own book is certainly one manifestation. Again, the ardour now shown in "Psychical Research," by the very distinguished, highly gifted, and cultivated men, who lead the society in London devoted to that object, is, to my inner convictions - knowing as I do something of the way the spiritual aspirations of the world are silently influenced by those whose work lies in that department of Nature - the obvious fruit of efforts, parallel to those with which I am more immediately concerned.

It only remains for me to disclaim, on behalf of the treatise which ensues, any pretension to high finish as regards the language in which it is cast. Longer familiarity with the vast and complicated scheme of cosmogony disclosed, will no doubt suggest improvements in the phraseology employed to expound it. Two years ago, neither I, nor any other European living, knew the alphabet of the science here for the first time put into a scientific shape - or subject at all events to an attempt in that direction - the science of Spiritual Causes and their Effects, of Super-physical Consciousness, of Cosmical Evolution. Though ideas had begun to offer themselves to the world in more or less embarrassing disguise of mystic symbology, no attempt had ever been made by any esoteric teacher, two years back, to put the doctrine forward in its plain abstract purity. As my own instruction progressed on those lines, I have had to coin phrases and suggest English words as equivalents for the ideas which were presented to my mind. I am by no means convinced that in all cases I have coined the best possible phrases and hit on the most neatly expressive words. For example, at the threshold of the subject we come upon the necessity of giving some name to the various elements or attributes of which the complete human creature is made up. "Element" would be an impossible word to use, on account of the confusion that would arise from its use in other significations; and the least objectionable on the whole seemed to me "principle," though to an ear trained in the niceties of metaphysical expression this word will have a very unsatisfactory sound in some of its present applications. Quite possibly, therefore, in process of time the Western nomenclature of the esoteric doctrine may be greatly developed in advance of that I have provisionally constructed. The Oriental nomenclature is far more elaborate, but metaphysical Sanskrit seems to be painfully embarrassing to a translator - the fault, my Indian friends assure me, not of Sanskrit, but of the language in which they are now required to express the Sanskrit ideal. Eventually we may find that, with the help of a little borrowing from familiar Greek quarries, English may prove more receptive of the new doctrine - or rather, of the primeval doctrine as newly disclosed - than has been supposed in the East.

# CHAPTER I

## Esoteric Teachers

The information contained in the following pages is no collection of inferences deduced from study. I am bringing to my readers knowledge which I have obtained by favour rather than by effort. It will not be found the less valuable on that account; I venture, on the contrary, to declare that it will be found of incalculably greater value, easily as I have obtained it, than any results in a similar direction which I could possibly have procured by ordinary methods of research, even had I possessed, in the highest degree, that which I make no claim to possess at all - Oriental scholarship.

Every one who has been concerned with Indian literature, and still more, any one who in India has taken interest in talking with cultivated Natives on philosophical subjects will be aware of a general conviction existing in the East that there are men living who know a great deal more about philosophy in the highest acceptation of the word - the science, the true knowledge of spiritual things, - than can be found recorded in any books. In Europe the notion of secrecy as applied to science is so repulsive to the prevailing instinct, that the first inclination of European thinkers is to deny the existence of that which they so much dislike. But circumstances have fully assured me during my residence in India that the conviction just referred to is perfectly well founded, and I have been privileged at last to receive a very considerable mass of instruction in the hitherto secret knowledge over which Oriental philosophers have brooded silently till now; instruction which has hitherto been only imparted to sympathetic students, prepared themselves to migrate into the camp of secrecy. Their teachers have been more than content that all other inquirers should be left in doubt as to whether there was anything of importance to learn at their hands.

With quite as much antipathy at starting as any one could have entertained to the old Oriental policy in regard to knowledge, I came, nevertheless, to perceive that the old Oriental knowledge itself was a very real and important possession. It may be excusable to regard the high grapes as sour so long as they are quite out of reach, but it would be foolish to persist in that opinion if a tall friend hands down a bunch and one finds them sweet.

For reasons that will appear as the present explanations proceed, the very considerable block of hitherto secret teaching this volume contains, has been conveyed to me, not only without conditions of the usual kind, but to the express end that I might convey it in my turn to the world at large.

Without the light of hitherto secret Oriental knowledge, it is impossible by any study of its published literature - English or Sanskrit - for students of even the most scholarly qualifications, to reach a comprehension of the inner doctrines and real meaning of any Oriental religion. This assertion conveys no reproach to the sympathetic, learned, and industrious writers of great ability who have studied Oriental religions generally, and Buddhism especially, in their external aspects. Buddhism, above all, is a religion which has enjoyed a dual existence from the very beginning of its introduction to the world. The real inner meaning of its doctrines has been kept back from uninitiated students, while the outer teachings have merely presented the multitude with a code of moral lessons and a veiled, symbolical literature, hinting at the existence of knowledge in the background.

This secret knowledge, in reality, long antedated the passage through earth-life of Gautama Buddha. Brahmin philosophy, in ages before Buddha, embodied the identical doctrine which may now be described as Esoteric Buddhism. Its outlines had indeed been blurred; its scientific form partially confused; but the general body of knowledge was already in possession of a select few before Buddha came to deal with it. Buddha, however, undertook the task of revising and refreshing the esoteric science of the inner circle of initiates, as well as the morality of the outer world. The circumstances under which this work was done, have been wholly misunderstood, nor would a straightforward explanation thereof be intelligible without explanations, which must first be furnished by a survey of the esoteric science itself.

From Buddha's time till now the esoteric science referred to has been jealously guarded as a precious heritage belonging exclusively to regularly initiated members of mysteriously organized associations. These, so far as Buddhism is concerned, are the Arahats, or more properly Arhats, referred to in Buddhist literature. They are the initiates who tread the "fourth path of holiness," spoken of in esoteric Buddhist writings. Mr Rhys Davids, referring to a multiplicity of original texts and Sanskrit authorities, says - "One might fill pages with the awe-struck and ecstatic praise which is lavished in Buddhist writings on this condition of mind, the fruit of the fourth path, the state of an Arahat, of a man made perfect according to the Buddhist faith." And then making a series of running quotations from Sanskrit authorities, he says - "To him who has finished the path and passed beyond sorrow, who has freed himself on all sides, thrown away every fetter, there is no more fever or grief....For such there are no more births....they are in the enjoyment of Nirvana. Their old karma is exhausted, no new karma is being produced; their hearts are free from the longing after future life, and no new yearnings springing up within them, they, the wise are extinguished like a lamp." These passages, and all like them, convey to European readers, at all events, an entirely false idea as to what sort of person an Arhat really is, as to the life he leads while on earth, and what he anticipates later on. But the elucidation of such points may be postponed for the moment. Some further passages from exoteric treatises may first be selected to show what an Arhat is generally supposed to be.

Mr Rhys Davids, speaking of Jhana and Samadhi - the belief that it was possible by intense self-absorption to attain supernatural faculties and powers - goes on to say - "So far as I am aware, no instance is recorded of any one, not either a member of the order, or a Brahmin ascetic, acquiring these powers. A Buddha always possessed them; whether Arahats as such, could work the particular miracles in question, and whether of mendicants, only Arahats or only Asekhas could do so, is at present not clear." Very little in the sources of information on the subject that have hitherto been explored will be found clear. But I am now merely endeavouring to show that Buddhist literature teems with allusions to the greatness and powers of the Arhats. For more intimate knowledge concerning them, special circumstances must furnish us with the required explanations.

Mr Arthur Lillie, in *Buddha and Early Buddhism*, tells us - "Six supernatural faculties were expected of the ascetic before he could claim the grade of Arhat. They are constantly alluded to in the Sutras as the six supernatural faculties, usually without further specification . . . .Man has a body composed of the four elements . . . . in this transitory body his intelligence is enchained, the ascetic finding himself thus confused, directs his mind to the creation of the Manas. He represents to himself, in thought, another body created from this material body - a body with a form, members, and organs. This body, in relation to the material body, is like the sword and the scabbard; or a serpent issuing from a basket in which it is confined. The ascetic then, purified and perfected, begins to practise supernatural faculties. He finds himself able to pass through material obstacles, walls, ramparts &c; he is able to throw his phantasmal appearance into many places at once . . . . he can leave this world and even reach the heaven of Brahma himself . . . . He acquires the power of hearing the sounds of the unseen world as distinctly as those of the phenomenal world - more distinctly in point of fact. Also by the power of Manas he is able to read the most secret thoughts of others, and to tell their characters." And so on with illustrations. Mr Lillie has not quite accurately divined the nature of the truth lying behind this popular version of the facts; but it is hardly necessary to quote more to show that the powers of the Arhats and their insight into spiritual things are respected by the world of Buddhism most profoundly, even though the Arhats themselves have been singularly indisposed to favour the world with autobiographies or scientific accounts of "the six supernatural powers."

A few sentences from Mr. Hoey's recent translation of Dr Oldenberg's "Budda: his Life, his Doctrine, his Order," may fall conveniently into this place, and then we may pass on. We read: - "Buddhist proverbial philosophy attributes in innumerable passages the possession of Nirvana to the saint who still treads the earth: 'The disciple who has put off lust and desire, rich in wisdom, has here on earth attained deliverance from death, the rest, the Nirvana, the eternal state. He who has escaped from the trackless hard mazes of the Sansara, who has crossed over and reached the shore, self-absorbed, without stumbling and without doubt, who has delivered himself from the earthly and attained Nirvana, him I call a true

Brahmin.' If the saint will even now put an end to his state of being he can do so, but the majority stand fast until Nature has reached her goal; of such may those words be said which are put in the mouth of the most prominent of Buddha's disciples, 'I long not for death; I long not for life; I wait till mine hour come, like a servant who awaiteth his reward.' "

A multiplication of such quotations would merely involve the repetition in various forms of exoteric conceptions concerning the Arhats. Like every fact or thought in Buddhism, the Arhat has two aspects, that in which he is presented to the world at large, and that in which he lives, moves, and has his being. In the popular estimation he is a saint waiting for a spiritual reward of the kind the populace can understand - a wonder-worker meanwhile by favour of supernatural agencies. In reality he is the longtried and proved-worthy custodian of the deepest and innermost philosophy of the one fundamental religion which Buddha refreshed and restored, and a student of natural science standing in the very foremost front of human knowledge, in regard not merely to the mysteries of spirit, but to the material constitution of the world as well.

Arhat is a Buddhist designation. That which is more familiar in India, where the attributes of Arhatship are not necessarily associated with professions of Buddhism, is Mahatma. With stories about the Mahatmas, India is saturated. The older Mahatmas are generally spoken of as Rishis; but the terms are interchangeable, and I have heard the title Rishi applied to men now living. All the attributes of the Arhats mentioned in Buddhist writings are described with no less reverence in Indian literature, as those of the Mahatmas, and this volume might be readily filled with translations of vernacular books, giving accounts of miraculous achievements by such of them as are known to history and tradition by name.

In reality, the Arhats and the Mahatmas are the same men. At that level of spiritual exaltation, supreme knowledge of the esoteric doctrine blends all original sectarian distinctions. By whatever name such illuminati may be called, they are the adepts of occult knowledge, sometimes spoken of in India now as the Brothers, and the custodians of the spiritual science which has been handed down to them by their predecessors.

We may search both ancient and modern literature in vain, however, for any systematic explanation of their doctrine or science. A good deal of this is dimly set forth in occult writing; but very little of this is of the least use to readers who take up the subject without previous knowledge acquired independently of books. It is under favour of direct instruction from one of their number that I am now enabled to attempt an outline of the Mahatmas' teaching, and it is in the same way that I have picked up what I know concerning the organization to which most of them, and the greatest, in the present day belong.

All over the world there are occultists of various degrees of eminence, and occult fraternities even, which have a great deal in common with the leading fraternity now established in Tibet. But all my inquiries into the subject have convinced me that the Tibetan Brotherhood is incomparably the highest of such associations, and regarded as such by all other associations - worthy of being looked upon themselves as really "enlightened" in the occult sense of the term. There are, it is true, many isolated mystics in India who are altogether self-taught and unconnected with occult bodies. Many of these will explain that they themselves attain to higher pinnacles of spiritual enlightenment than the Brothers of Tibet, or any other people on earth. But the examination of such claims in all cases I have encountered, would, I think, lead any impartial outsider, however little qualified himself by personal development to be a judge of occult enlightenment, to the conclusion that they are altogether unfounded. I know one native of India, for example, a man of European education, holding a high appointment under Government, of good station in society, most elevated character, and enjoying unusual respect with such Europeans as are concerned with him in official life, who will only accord to the Brothers of Tibet a second place in the world of spiritual enlightenment. The first place he regards as occupied by one person, now in this world no longer - his own occult master in life - whom he resolutely asserts to have been in incarnation of the Supreme Being. His own (my friend's) inner senses were so awakened by this Master, that the visions of his entranced state, into which he can still throw himself at will, are to him the only spiritual region in which he can feel interested. Convinced that the Supreme Being was his personal instructor from the beginning, and continues so still in the subjective state, he is naturally inaccessible to suggestions that his impressions may be distorted by reason of his own misdirected psychological development. Again, the highly cultivated devotees, to be met with occasionally in India, who build up a conception of Nature, the universe, and God, entirely on a metaphysical basis, and who have evolved their systems by sheer force of transcendental thinking, will take some established system of philosophy as its groundwork, and amplify on this to an extent which only an Oriental metaphysician could dream of. They win disciples who put implicit faith in them, and found their little school which flourishes for a time within its own limits; but speculative philosophy of such a kind is rather occupation for the mind than knowledge. Such "Masters," by comparison with the organized adepts of the highest brotherhood, are like rowing-boats compared with ocean steamships - helpful conveyances on their own native lake or river, but not craft to whose protection you can trust yourself on a world-wide voyage of exploration over the sea.

Descending lower again in the scale, we find India dotted all over with Yogis and Fakirs, in all stages of self-development, from that of dirty savages, but little elevated above the gipsy fortune-tellers of an English racecourse, to men whose seclusion a stranger will find it very difficult to penetrate, and whose abnormal faculties and powers need only be seen or experienced to shatter the incredulity of the most contented representative of modern Western scepticism. Careless inquirers are very apt to confound such persons with the great adepts of whom they may vaguely hear.

Concerning the real adepts, meanwhile, I cannot at present venture on any account of what the Tibetan organization is like, as regards its highest ruling authorities. Those Mahatmas themselves, of whom some more or less adequate conception may, perhaps, be formed by readers who will follow me patiently to the end, are subordinate by several degrees to the chief of all. Let us deal rather with the earlier conditions of occult training, which can more easily be grasped.

The level of elevation which constitutes a man - what the outer world calls a Mahatma or "Brother" - is only attained after prolonged and weary probation, and anxious ordeals of really terrible severity. One may find people who have spent twenty or thirty years or more, in blameless and arduous devotion to the life-task on which they have entered, and are still in the earlier degrees of chelaship, still looking up to the heights of adeptship as far above their heads. And at whatever age a boy or man dedicates himself to the occult career, he dedicates himself to it, be it remembered, without any reservations and for life. The task he undertakes is the development in himself of a great many faculties and attributes which are so utterly dormant in ordinary mankind, that their very existence is unsuspected - the possibility of their development denied. And these faculties and attributes must be developed by the chela himself, with very little, if any, help, beyond guidance and direction from his master. "The adept." says an occult aphorism, "becomes: he is not made." One may illustrate this point by reference to a very common-place physical exercise. Every man living, having the ordinary use of his limbs, is qualified to swim. But put those who, as the common phrase goes, cannot swim, into deep water, and they will struggle and be drowned. The mere way to move the limbs is no mystery; but unless the swimmer in moving them has a full belief that such movement will produce the required result, the required result is not produced. In this case, we are dealing with mechanical forces merely, but the same principle runs up into dealings with subtler forces. Very much further than people generally imagine will mere "confidence" carry the occult neophyte. How many European readers, who would be quite incredulous if told of some results which occult chelas in the most incipient stages of their training have to accomplish by sheer force of confidence, hear constantly in church nevertheless, the familiar Biblical assurances of the power which resides in faith, and let the words pass by like the wind, leaving no impression.

The great end and purpose of adeptship is the achievement of spiritual development, the nature of which is only veiled and disguised by the common phrases of exoteric language. That the adept seeks to unite his soul with God, that he may thereby pass into Nirvana, is a statement that conveys no definite meaning to the ordinary reader, and the more he examines it with the help of ordinary books and methods, the less likely will he be to realize the nature of the process contemplated, or of the condition desired. It will be necessary to deal first with the esoteric conception of Nature, and the origin and destinies of Man, which differ widely from theological conceptions, before an explanation of the aim which the adept pursues can become intelligible. Meanwhile, however, it is desirable, at the very outset, to disabuse the reader of one misconception in regard to the objects of adeptship that he may very likely have framed.

The development of those spiritual faculties, whose culture has to do with the highest objects of the occult life, gives rise, as it progresses, to a great deal of incidental knowledge, having to do with the physical laws of Nature not yet generally understood. This knowledge, and the practical art of manipulating certain obscure forces of Nature, which it brings in its train, invest an adept, and even an adept's pupils, at a comparatively early stage of their education, with very extraordinary powers, the application of which to matters of daily life will sometimes produce results that seem altogether miraculous; and, from the ordinary point of view, the acquisition of apparently miraculous power is such a stupendous achievement, that people are sometimes apt to fancy that the adept's object in seeking the knowledge he attains has been to invest himself with these coveted powers. It would be as reasonable to say of any great patriot of military history that his object in becoming a soldier had been to wear a gay uniform and impress the imagination of the nursemaids.

The Oriental method of cultivating knowledge has always differed diametrically from that pursued in the West during the growth of modern science. Whilst Europe has investigated Nature as publicly as possible, every step being discussed with the utmost freedom, and every fresh fact acquired, circulated at once for the benefit of all, Asiatic science has been studied secretly and its conquests jealously guarded. I need not as yet attempt either criticism or defence of its methods. But at all events these methods have been relaxed to some extent in my own case, and, as already stated, it is with the full consent of my teachers that I now follow the bent of my own inclinations as a European, and communicate what I have learned to all who may be willing to receive it. Later on it will be seen how the departure from the ordinary rules of occult study embodied in the concessions now made, falls naturally into its place in the whole scheme of occult philosophy. The approaches to that philosophy have always been open, in one sense, to all. Vaguely throughout the world in various ways has been diffused the idea that some process of study which men here and there did actually follow, might lead to the acquisition of a higher kind of knowledge than that taught to mankind at large in books or by public religious preachers. The East, as pointed out, has always been more than vaguely impressed with this belief, but even in the West the whole block of symbolical literature relating to astrology, alchemy, and mysticism generally has fermented in European society, carrying to some few peculiarly receptive and qualified minds the conviction that behind all this superficially meaningless nonsense great truths lay concealed. For such persons eccentric study has sometimes revealed hidden passages leading to the grandest imaginable realms of enlightenment. But till now, in all such cases, in accordance with the law of those schools, the neophyte no sooner forced his way into the region of mystery than he was bound over to the most inviolable secrecy as to everything connected with his entrance and further progress there. In Asia in the same way, the "chela," or pupil of occultism, no sooner became a chela than he ceased to be a witness on behalf of the reality of occult knowledge. I have been astonished to find, since my own connection with the subject, how numerous such chelas are. But it is impossible to imagine any human act more improbable than the unauthorized revelation by any such chela, to persons in the outer world, that he is one, and so the great esoteric school of philosophy successfully guards its seclusion.

In a former book, "The Occult World," I have given a full and straightforward narrative of the circumstances under which I came in contact with the gifted and deeply instructed men from whom I have since obtained the teaching this volume contains. I need not repeat the story. I now come forward prepared to deal with the subject in a new way. The existence of occult adepts, and the importance of their acquirements, may be established along two different lines of argument: firstly, by means of external evidence, - the testimony of qualified witnesses, the manifestation by or through persons connected with adepts, of abnormal faculties affording more than a presumption of abnormally enlarged knowledge; secondly, by the presentation of such a considerable portion of this knowledge as may convey intrinsic assurances of its own value. My first book proceeded by the former method; I now approach the more formidable task of working on the latter.

Annotations

The further we advance in occult study, the more exalted in many ways become our conceptions of the Mahatmas. The complete comprehension of the manner in which these persons become differentiated from human kind at large, is not to be achieved by the help of mere intellectual effort. These are aspects of the adept nature which have to do with the extraordinary development of the higher principles in man, which cannot be realized by the application of the lower. But while crude conceptions in the beginning thus fall very short of reaching the real level of the facts, a curious complication of the problem arises in this way. Our first idea of an adept who has achieved the power of penetrating the tremendous secrets of spiritual nature, is modelled on our conception of a very highly gifted man of science on our own plane. We are apt to think of him as once an adept always an adept, - as a very exalted human being, who must necessarily bring into play in all the relations of his life the attributes that attach to him as a Mahatma. In this way while - as above pointed out - we shall certainly fail, do all we can, to do justice in our thoughts to his attributes as a Mahatma, we may very easily run to the opposite extreme in our thinking about him in his ordinary human aspect, and thus land ourselves in many perplexities, as we acquire a partial familiarity with the characteristics of the occult world. It is just because the highest attributes of adeptship have to do with principles in human nature which quite transcend the limits of physical existence, that the adept or Mahatma can only be such in the highest acceptation of the word, when he is, as the phrase goes, "out of the body," or at all events thrown by special efforts of his will into an abnormal condition. When he is not called upon to make such efforts or to pass entirely beyond the limitations of this fleshly prison, he is much more like an ordinary man than experience of him in some of his aspects would lead his disciples to believe.

A correct appreciation of this state of things explains the apparent contradiction involved in the position of the occult pupil towards his masters, as compared with some of the declarations that the master himself will frequently put forward. For example, the Mahatmas are persistent in asserting that they are not infallible, that they are men, like the rest of us, perhaps with a somewhat more enlarged comprehension of nature than the generality of mankind, but still liable to err both in the direction of practical business with which they may be concerned, and in their estimate of the characters of other men, or the capacity of candidates for occult development. But how are we to reconcile statements of this nature with the fundamental principle at the bottom of all occult research which enjoins the neophyte to put his trust in the teaching and guidance of his master absolutely and without reserve? The solution of the difficulty is found in the state of things above referred to. While the adept may be a man quite surprisingly liable to err sometimes in the manipulation of worldly business, just as with ourselves some of the greatest men of genius are liable to make mistakes in their daily life that matter-of-fact people would never commit, on the other hand, directly a Mahatma comes to deal with the higher mysteries of spiritual science, he does so by virtue of the exercise of his Mahatma-attributes, and in dealing with these can hardly be recognized as liable to err.

This consideration enables us to feel that the trustworthiness of the teachings derived from such a source as those which have inspired the present volume, is altogether above the reach of small incidents which in the progress of our experience may seem to claim a revision of that enthusiastic confidence in the supreme wisdom of the adepts which the first approaches to occult study will generally evoke.

Not that such enthusiasm or reverence will really be *diminished* on the part of any occult chela as his comprehension of the world he is entering expands. The man who in one of his aspects is a Mahatma, may rather be brought within the limits of affectionate human regard, than deprived of his claims to reverence, by the consideration that in his ordinary life he is not so utterly lifted above the common-place run of human feeling as some of his Nirvanic experiences might lead us to believe that he would be.

If we keep constantly in mind that an adept is only truly an adept when exercising adept functions but that when exercising adept functions, but that when exercising these he may soar into spiritual rapport with that which is, in regard at all events to the limitations of our solar system, all that we practically mean by omniscience, we shall then be guarded from many of the mistakes that the embarrassments of the subject might create.

Intricacies concerning the nature of the adept may be noticed here, which will hardly be quite intelligible without reference to some later chapters of this book, but which have so important a bearing on all attempts to understand what adeptship is really like that it may be convenient to deal with them at once. The dual nature of the Mahatma is so complete that some of his influence or wisdom on the higher planes of nature may actually be drawn upon by those in peculiar psychic relations with him, without the Mahatma-man being at the moment even conscious that such an appeal has been made to him. In this way it becomes open to us to speculate on the possibility that the relation between the spiritual Mahatma and the Mahatma-man may sometimes be rather in the nature of what is sometimes spoken of in esoteric writing as an overshadowing than as an incarnation in the complete sense of the word.

Furthermore as another independent complication of the matter we reach this fact, that each Mahatma is not merely a human ego in a very exalted state, but belongs, so to speak, to some specific department in the great economy of nature. Every adept must belong to one or other of seven great types of adeptship, but although we may almost certainly infer that correspondences might be traced between these various types and the seven principles of man, I should shrink myself from attempting a complete elucidation of this hypothesis. It will be enough to apply the idea to what we know vaguely of the occult organization in its higher regions. For some time past it has been affirmed in esoteric writing that there are five great Chohans or superior Mahatmas presiding over the whole body of the adept fraternity. When the foregoing chapter of this book was written, I was under the impression that one supreme chief on a different level again exercised authority over these five Chohans, but it now appears to me that this personage may rather be regarded as a sixth Chohan, himself the head of the sixth type of Mahatmas, and this conjecture leads at once to the further inference that there must be a seventh Chohan to complete the correspondences which we thus discern. But just as the seventh principle in nature or in man is a conception of the most intangible order eluding the grasp of any intellectual thinking, and only describable in shadowy phrases of metaphysical non-significance, so we may be quite sure that the seventh Chohan is very unapproachable by untrained imaginations. But even he no doubt plays a part in what may be called the higher economy of spiritual nature, and that there is such a personage visible occasionally to some of the other Mahatmas I take to be the case. But speculation concerning him is valuable chiefly as helping to give consistency to the idea above thrown out, according to which the Mahatmas may be comprehended in their true aspect as necessary phenomena of nature without whom the evolution of humanity could hardly be imagined as advancing, not as merely the exceptional men who have attained great spiritual exaltation.

# CHAPTER II

## The Constitution of Man

A survey of Cosmogony, as comprehended by occult science, must precede any attempt to explain the means by which a knowledge of that cosmogony itself has been acquired. The methods of esoteric research have grown out of natural facts, with which exoteric science is wholly unacquainted. These natural facts are concerned with the premature development in occult adepts of faculties, which mankind at large has not yet evolved; and these faculties, in turn, enable their possessors to explore the mysteries of Nature, and verify the esoteric doctrines, setting forth its grand design. The practical student of occultism may develop the faculties first and apply them to the observation of Nature afterwards, but the exhibition of the theory of Nature for Western readers merely seeking its intellectual comprehension, must precede consideration of the inner senses, which occult research employs. On the other hand, a survey of cosmogony, as comprehended by occult science, could only be scientifically arranged at the expense of intelligibility for European readers. To begin at the beginning, we should endeavour to realize the state of the universe before evolution sets in. This subject is by no means shirked by esoteric students, and later on, in the course of this sketch, some hints will be given concerning the views occultism entertains of the earlier processes through which cosmic matter passes on its way to evolution. But an orderly statement of the earliest processes of Nature would embody references to man's spiritual constitution, which would not be understood without some preliminary explanation.

Seven distinct principles are recognized by esoteric science, as entering into the constitution of man. The classification differs so widely from any with which European readers will be familiar that I shall naturally be asked for the grounds on which occultism reaches so far-fetched a conclusion. But I must, on account of inherent peculiarities in the subject, which will be comprehended later on, beg for this Oriental knowledge I am bringing home, a hearing (in the first instance at all events) of the Oriental kind. The Oriental and the European systems of conveying knowledge are as unlike as any two methods can be. The West pricks and piques the learner's controversial instinct at every step. He is encouraged to dispute and resist conviction. He is forbidden to take any scientific statement on authority. *Pari Passu*, as he acquires knowledge, he must learn how that knowledge has been acquired, and he is made to feel that no fact is worth knowing, unless he knows, with it, the way to prove it a fact. The East manages its pupils on a wholly different plan. It no more disregards the necessity of proving its teaching than the West, but it provides proof of a wholly different sort. It enables the student to search Nature for himself, and verify its teachings, in those regions which Western philosophy can only invade by speculation and argument. It never takes the trouble to argue about anything. It says: - "So and so is fact; here is the key of knowledge; now go and see for yourself." In this way it comes to pass that teaching per se is never anything else but teaching on authority. Teaching and proof do not go hand in hand; they follow one another in due order. A further consequence of this method is that Eastern philosophy employs the method which we in the West have discarded for good reasons as incompatible with our own line of intellectual development - the system of reasoning from generals to particulars. The purposes which European science usually has in view would certainly not be answered by that plan, but I think that any one who goes far in the present inquiry will feel that the system of reasoning up from the details of knowledge to general inferences is inapplicable to the work in hand. One cannot understand details in this department of knowledge till we get a general understanding of the whole scheme of things. Even to convey this general comprehension by mere language, is a large and by no means an easy task. To pause at every moment of the exposition in order to collect what separate evidence may be available for the proof of each separate statement, would be practically impossible. Such a method would break down the patience of the reader, and prevent him from deriving, as he may from a more condensed treatise, that definite conception as to what the esoteric doctrine means to teach, which it is my business to evoke.

This reflection may suggest, in passing, a new view, having an intimate connection with our present subject, of the Platonic and Aristotelian systems of reasoning. Plato's system, roughly described as reasoning from universals to particulars, is condemned by modern habits in favour of the later and exactly inverse system. But Plato was in fetters in attempting to defend his system. There is every reason to believe that his familiarity with esoteric science prompted his method, and that the usual restrictions under which he laboured as an initiated occultist, forbade him from saying as much as would really justify it. No one can study even as much occult science as this volume contains, and then turn to Plato or even to any intelligent epitome of Plato's system of thought, without finding correspondences cropping out at every turn.

The higher principles of the series which go to constitute Man are not fully developed in the mankind with which we are as yet familiar, but a complete or perfect man would be resolvable into the following elements. To facilitate the application of these explanations to ordinary exoteric Buddhist writings the Sanskrit names of these principles are given as well as suitable terms in English. [The nomenclature here adopted differs slightly from that hit upon when some of the present teachings were first given out in a fragmentary form in the Theosophist. Later on it will be seen that the names now preferred embody a fuller conception of the whole system, and avoid some difficulties to which the earlier names give rise. If the earlier presentations of esoteric science were thus imperfect, one can hardly be surprised at so natural a consequence of the difficulties under which its English exponents laboured. But no substantial errors have to be confessed or deplored. The connotations of the present names are more accurate than those of the phrases first selected, but the explanations originally given, as far as they went, were quite in harmony with those now developed.].

| | | |
|---|---|---|
| 1 | The Body | *Rupa* |
| 2 | Vitality | *Prana*, or *Jiva* |
| 3 | Astral Body | *Linga Sharira* |
| 4 | Animal Soul | *Kama Rupa* |
| 5 | Human Soul | *Manas* |
| 6 | Spiritual Soul | *Buddhi* |
| 7 | Spirit | *Atma* |

Directly conceptions, so transcendental as some of those included in this analysis, are set forth in a tabular statement, they seem to incur certain degradation, against which, in endeavouring to realize clearly what is meant, we must be ever on our guard. Certainly it would be impossible for even the most skilful professor of occult science to exhibit each of these principles separate and distinct from the others, as the physical elements of a compound body can be separated by analysis and preserved independently of each other. The elements of a physical body are all on the same plane of materiality, but the elements of man are on very different planes. The finest gases of which the body may to some extent be chemically composed, are still, on one scale at all events, on nearly the lowest level of materiality. The second principle which, by its union with gross matter, changes if from what we generally call inorganic, or what might more properly be called inert, into living matter, is at once a something different from the finest example of matter in its lower state. Is the second principle then anything that we can truly call matter at all? The question lands us, thus, at the very outset of this inquiry, in the middle of the subtle metaphysical discussion as to whether force and matter are different or identical. Enough for the moment to state that occult science regards them as identical, and that it contemplates no principle in Nature as wholly immaterial. In this way, though no conceptions of the universe, of man's destiny, or of Nature generally, are more spiritual than those of occult science, that science is wholly free from the logical error of attributing material results to immaterial causes. The esoteric doctrine is thus really the missing link between materialism and spirituality.

The clue to the mystery involved, lies of course in the fact, directly cognizable by occult experts, that matter exists in other states besides those which are cognizable by the five senses.

The second principle of Man, Vitality, thus consists of matter in its aspect as force, and its affinity for the grosser state of matter is so great that it cannot be separated from any given particle or mass of this, except by instantaneous translation to some other particle or mass. When a man's body dies, by desertion of the higher principles which have rendered it a living reality, the second, or life principle, no longer a unity itself, is nevertheless inherent still in the particles of the body as this decomposes, attaching itself to other organisms to which that very process of decomposition gives rise. Bury the body in the earth and its jiva will attach itself to the vegetation which springs above, or the lower animal forms which evolve from its substance. Burn the body, and indestructible jiva flies back none the less instantaneously to the body of the planet itself from which it was originally borrowed, entering into some new combination as its affinities may determine.

The third principle, the Astral Body or Linga Sharira, is an ethereal duplicate of the physical body, its original design. It guides jiva in its work on the physical particles, and causes it to build up the shape which these assume. Vitalized itself by the higher principles, its unity is only preserved by the union of the whole group. At death it is disembodied for a brief period, and, under some abnormal conditions, may even be temporarily visible to the external sight of still living persons. Under such conditions it is taken of course for the ghost of the departed person. Spectral apparitions may sometimes be occasioned in other ways, but the third principle, when *that* results in a visible phenomenon, is a mere aggregation of molecules in a peculiar state, having no life or consciousness of any kind whatever. It is no more a Being, than any cloud wreath in the sky which happens to settle into the semblance of some animal form. Broadly speaking, the linga sharira never leaves the body except at death, nor migrates far from the body even in that case. When seen at all, and this can but rarely occur, it can only be seen near where the physical body still lies. In some very peculiar cases of spiritualistic mediumship, it may for a short time exude from the physical body and be visible near it, but the medium in such cases stands the while in considerable danger of his life. Disturb unwillingly the conditions under which the linga sharira was set free, and its return might be impeded. The second principle would then soon cease to animate the physical body as a unity, and death would ensue.

During the last year or two, while hints and scraps of occult science have been finding their way out into the world, the expression, "Astral Body," has been applied to a certain semblance of the human form, fully inhabited by its higher principles, which can migrate to any distance from the physical body - projected consciously and with exact intention by a living adept, or unintentionally, by the accidental application of certain mental forces to his loosened principles, by any person at the moment of death. For ordinary purposes there is no practical inconvenience in using the expression "Astral Body" for the appearance to projected - indeed, any more strictly accurate expression, as will be seen directly, would be cumbersome, and we must go on using the phrase in both meanings. No confusion need arise; but, strictly speaking, the linga sharira, or third principle, is the astral body, and that cannot be sent about as the vehicle of the higher principles.

The three lower principles, it will be seen, are altogether of the earth, perishable in their nature as a single entity, though indestructible as regards their molecules, and absolutely done with by man at his death.

The fourth principle is the first of those which belong to man's higher nature. The Sanskrit designation, *kama rupa*, is often translated "Body of Desire," which seems rather a clumsy and inaccurate form of words. A closer translation, having regard to meanings rather than words, would, perhaps, be "Vehicle of Will," but the name already adopted above, Animal Soul, may be more accurately suggestive still.

In the Theosophist for October, 1881, when the first hints about the septenary constitution of man were given out, the fifth principle was called the animal soul, as contra-distinguished from the sixth or "spiritual soul;" but though this nomenclature sufficed to mark the required distinction, it degraded the fifth principle, which is essentially the human principle. Though humanity is animal in its nature as compared with spirit, it is elevated above the correctly defined animal creation in every other aspect. By introducing a new name for the fifth principle, we are enabled to throw back the designation "animal soul" to its proper place. This arrangement need not interfere, meanwhile, with an appreciation of the way in which the fourth principle is the seat of that will or desire to which the Sanskrit name refers. And, withal, the *kama rupa* is the animal soul, the highest *developed* principle of the brute creation, susceptible of evolution into something far higher by its union with the growing fifth principle in man, but still the animal soul which man is by no means yet without, the seat of all animal desires, and a potent force in the human body as well, pressing upwards, so to speak, as well as downwards, and capable of influencing the fifth, for practical purposes, as well as of being influenced by the fifth for its own control and improvement.

The fifth principle, human soul, or Manas (as described in Sanskrit in one of its aspects), is the seat of reason and *memory*. It is a portion of this principle, animated by the fourth, which is really projected to distant places by an adept, when he makes an appearance in what is commonly called his astral body.

Now the fifth principle, or human soul, in the majority of mankind is not even yet fully developed. This fact about the imperfect development as yet of the higher principles is very important. We cannot get a correct conception of the present place of man in Nature if we make the mistake of regarding him as a fully perfected being already. And that mistake would be fatal to any reasonable anticipations concerning the future that awaits him - fatal also to any appreciation of the appropriateness of the future which the esoteric doctrine explains to us as actually awaiting him. Since the fifth principle is not yet fully developed, it goes without saying that the sixth principle is still in embryo. This idea has been variously indicated in recent forecasts of the great doctrine. Sometimes it has been said, we do not truly possess any sixth principle, we merely have germs of a sixth principle. It has also been said, the sixth principle is not in us; it hovers over us; it is a something that the highest aspirations of our nature must work up towards. But it is also said: - All things, not man alone, but every animal, plant, and mineral have their seven principles, and the highest principles of all - the seventh itself - vitalizes that continuous thread of life which runs all through evolution, uniting into a definite succession, the almost innumerable incarnations of that one life which constitute a complete series. We must imbibe all these various conceptions and weld them together, or extract their essence, to learn the doctrine of the sixth principle. Following the order of ideas which just now suggested the application of the term animal soul to the fourth principle, and human soul to the fifth, the sixth may be called the spiritual soul of man, and the seventh, therefore, spirit itself.

In another aspect of the idea the sixth principle may be called the vehicle of the seventh, and the fourth the vehicle of the fifth; but yet another mode of dealing with the problem teaches us to regard each of the higher principles from the fourth upwards, as a vehicle of what, in Buddhist philosophy, is called the One Life or Spirit. According to this view of the matter of one life is that which perfects, by inhabiting the various vehicles. In the animal the one life is concentrated in the *kama rupa*. In man it begins to penetrate the fifth principle as well. In perfected man it penetrates the sixth, and when it penetrates the seventh, man ceases to be man, and attains a wholly superior condition of existence.

This latter view of the position is especially valuable as guarding against the notion that the four higher principles are like a bundle of sticks tied together, but each having individualities of their own if untied. Neither the animal soul alone, nor the spiritual soul alone, has any individuality at all; but, on the other hand, the fifth principle would be incapable of separation from the others in such a way, that its individuality would be preserved while both the deserted principles would be left unconscious. It has been said that the finer principles themselves even, are material and molecular in their constitution, though composed of a higher order of matter than the physical senses can take note of. So they are separable, and the sixth principle itself can be imagined as divorcing itself from its lower neighbour. But in that state of separation, and at this stage of mankind's development, it could simply reincarnate itself in such an emergency, and grow a new fifth principle by contact with a human organism; in such a case, the fifth principle would lean upon and become one with the fourth, and be proportionately degraded. And yet this fifth principle, which cannot stand alone, is the personality of the man; and its cream, in union with the sixth, his continuous individuality through successive lives.

The circumstances and attractions under the influence of which the principles do divide up, and the manner in which the consciousness of man is dealt with then, will be discussed later on. Meanwhile, a better understanding of the whole position than could ensue from a continued prosecution of the inquiry on these lines now, will be obtained by turning first to the processes of evolution by means of which the principles of man have been developed.

## Annotations

Some objection has been raised to the method in which the Esoteric Doctrine is presented to the reader in this book, on the ground that it is materialistic. I doubt if in any other way the ideas to be dealt with could so well be brought within the grasp of the mind, but it is easy, when they once are grasped, to translate them into terms of idealism. The higher principles will be the better susceptible of treatment as so many different states of the Ego, when the attributes of these states have been separately considered as principles undergoing evolution. But it may be useful to dwell for awhile on the view of the human constitution according to which the consciousness of the entity migrates successively through the stages of development, which the different principles represent.

In the highest evolution we need concern ourselves with at present - that of the perfected Mahatma - it is sometimes asserted in occult teaching that the consciousness of the Ego has acquired the power of residing altogether in the sixth principle. But it would be a gross view of the subject, and erroneous, to suppose that the Mahatma has on that account shaken off altogether, like a discarded sheath or sheaths, the fourth and fifth principles, in which his consciousness may have been seated during an earlier stage of his evolution. The entity, which was the fourth or fifth principle before, has come now to be different in its attributes, and to be entirely divorced from certain tendencies or dispositions, and is therefore a sixth principle. The change can be spoken of in more general terms as an emancipation of the adept's nature from the enthralments of his lower self, from desires of the ordinary earth-life - even from the limitations of the affections; for the Ego, which is entirely conscious in his sixth principle, has realized the unity of the true Egos of all mankind on the higher plane, and can no longer be drawn by bonds of sympathy to any one more than to any other. He has attained that love of humanity as a whole which transcends the love of the *Maya* or illusion which constitutes the separate human creature for the limited being on the lower levels of evolution. He has not lost his fourth and fifth principles, - these have themselves attained Mahatmaship; just as the animal soul of the lower kingdom, in reaching humanity, has blossomed into the fifth state. That consideration helps us to realize more accurately the passage of ordinary human beings through the long series of incarnations of the human plane. Once fairly on that plane of existence the consciousness of the primitive man gradually envelopes the attributes of the fifth principle. But the Ego at first remains a centre of thought activity working chiefly with impulses and desires of the fourth stage of evolution. Flashes of the higher human reason illumine it fitfully at first, but by degrees the more intellectual man grows into the fuller possession of this.

The impulses of human reason assert themselves more and more strongly. The invigorated mind becomes the predominant force in the life. Consciousness is transferred to the fifth principle, oscillating, however, between the tendencies of the lower and higher nature for a long while - that is to say, over vast periods of evolution and many hundred lives, - and thus gradually purifying and exalting the Ego. All this while the Ego is thus a unity in one aspect of the matter, and its sixth principle but a potentiality of ultimate development. As regards the seventh principle, that is the true Unknowable, the supreme controlling cause of all things, which is the same for one man as for every man, the same for humanity as for the animal kingdom, the same for the physical as for the astral or devachanic or nirvanic planes of existence. No one man has got a seventh principle, in the higher conception of the subject: we are all in the same unfathomable way overshadowed by the *seventh* principle of the cosmos.

How does this view of the subject harmonize with the statement in the foregoing chapter, that in a certain sense the principles are separable, and that the sixth even can be imagined as divorcing itself from its next lower neighbour, and, by reincarnation, as growing a new fifth principle by contact with a human organism? There is no incompatibility in the spirit of the two views. The seventh principle is one and indivisible in all Nature, but there is a mysterious persistence through it of certain life impulses, which thus constitute threads on which successive existences may be strung. Such a life impulse does not expire even in the extraordinary case supposed, in which an Ego, projected upon it and developed along it to a certain point, falls away from it altogether and as a complete whole. I am not in a position to dogmatize with precision as to what happens in such a case, but the subsequent incarnations of the spirit along that line of impulse are clearly of the original sequence; and thus, in the materialistic treatment of the idea, it may be said, with as much approach to accuracy as language will allow in either mode, that the sixth principle of the fallen entity in such a case separates itself from the original fifth, and reincarnates on its own account.

But with these abnormal processes it is unnecessary to occupy ourselves to any great extent. The normal evolution is the problem we have first to solve; and while the consideration of the seven principles as such is, to my own mind, the most instructive method by which the problem can be dealt with, it is well to remember always that the Ego is a unity progressing through various spheres or states of being, undergoing change and growth and purification all through the course of its evolution, - that it is a consciousness seated in this, or that, or the other, of the potential attributes of a human entity.

# CHAPTER III

## The Planetary Chain

Esoteric science, though the most spiritual system imaginable, exhibits as running throughout Nature, the most exhaustive system of evolution that the human mind can conceive. The Darwinian theory of evolution is simply an independent discovery of a portion - unhappily but a small portion - of the vast natural truth. But occultists know how to explain evolution without degrading the highest principles of man. The esoteric doctrine finds itself under no obligation to keep its science and religion in separate water-tight compartments. Its theory of physics and its theory of spirituality are not only reconcilable with each other, they are intimately blended together and interdependent. And the first great fact which occult science presents to our notice in reference to the origin of man on this globe, will be seen to help the imagination over some serious embarrassments of the familiar scientific idea of evolution. The evolution of man is not a process carried out on this planet alone. It is a result to which many worlds in different conditions of material and spiritual development have contributed. If this statement were merely put forward as a conjecture, it would surely recommend itself forcibly to rational minds. For there is a manifest irrationality in the commonplace notion that man's existence is divided into a material beginning, lasting sixty or seventy years, and a spiritual remainder lasting for ever. The irrationality amounts to absurdity when it is alleged that the acts of the sixty or seventy years - the blundering, helpless acts of ignorant human life - are permitted by the perfect justice of an all-wise Providence to define the conditions of that later life of infinite duration. Nor is it less extravagant to imagine that, apart from the question of justice, the life beyond the grave should be exempt from the law of change, progress, and improvement, which every analogy of Nature points to as probably running through all the varied existences of the universe. But once abandon the idea of a uniform, unvarying, unprogressive life beyond the grave - once admit the conception of change and progress in that life - and we admit the idea of a variety hardly compatible with any other hypothesis than that of progress through successive worlds. As we have said before, this is not a hypothesis at all for occult science, but a fact, ascertained and verified beyond the reach (for occultists) of doubt or contradiction.

The life and evolutionary processes of this planet - in fact, all which constitutes it something more than a dead lump of chaotic matter - are linked with the life and evolutionary processes of several other planets. But let it not be supposed that there is no finality as regards the scheme of this planetary union to which we belong. The human imagination once set free is apt sometimes to bound too far. Once let this notion, that the earth is merely one link in a mighty chain of worlds, be fully accepted as probable, or true, and it may suggest the whole starry heavens as the heritage of the human family. That idea would involve a serious misconception. One globe does not afford Nature scope for the processes by which mankind has been evoked from chaos, but these processes do not require more than a limited and definite number of globes. Separated as these are, in regard to the gross mechanical matter of which they consist, they are closely and intimately bound together by subtle currents and forces, whose existence reason need not be much troubled to concede, since the existence of some connection - of force or ethereal media - uniting all visible celestial bodies, is proved by the mere fact that they are visible. It is along these subtle currents that the life elements pass from world to world.

The fact, however, will at once be liable to distortion, to suit preconceived habits of mind. Some readers may imagine our meaning to be that after death the surviving soul will be drawn into the currents of that world with which its affinities connect it. The real process is more methodical. The system of worlds is a circuit round which *all* individual spiritual entities have alike to pass; and that passage constitutes the Evolution of Man. For it must be realized that the evolution of man is a process still going on, and by no means yet complete. Darwinian writings have taught the modern world to regard the ape as an ancestor, but the simple conceit of Western speculation has rarely permitted European evolutionists to look in the other direction, and recognize the probability, that to our remote descendants we may be, as that unwelcome progenitor to us. Yet the two facts just declared hinge together. The higher evolution will be accomplished by our progress through the successive worlds of the system; and in higher forms we shall return to this earth again and again. But the avenues of thought through which we look forward to this prospect, are of almost inconceivable length.

It will readily be supposed that the chain of worlds to which this earth belongs are not all prepared for a material existence exactly, or even approximately resembling our own. There would be no meaning in an organized chain of worlds which were all alike, and might as well all have been amalgamated into one. In reality the worlds with which we are connected are very unlike each other, not merely in outward conditions, but in that supreme characteristic, the proportion in which spirit and matter are mingled in their constitution. Our own world presents us with conditions in which spirit and matter are on the whole evenly balanced in equilibrium. Let it not be supposed on that account that it is very highly elevated in the scale of perfection. On the contrary, it occupies a very low place in that scale. The worlds that are higher in the scale are those in which spirit largely predominates. There is another world attached to the chain, rather than forming a part of it, in which matter asserts itself even more decisively than on earth, but this may be spoken of later.

That the superior worlds which man may come to inhabit in his onward progress should gradually become more and more spiritual in their constitution - life there being more and more successfully divorced from gross material needs - will seem reasonable enough at the first glance. But the first glance in imagination at those which might conversely be called the inferior, but may with less inaccuracy be spoken of as the preceding worlds, would perhaps suggest that they ought to be conversely less spiritual, more material, than this earth. The fact is quite the other way, and must be so, it will be seen on reflection, in a chain of worlds which is an endless chain - i.e. round and round which the evolutionary process travels. If that process had merely one journey to travel along a path which never returned into itself, one could think of it, at any rate, as working from almost absolute matter up to almost absolute spirit; but Nature works always in complete curves, and travels always in paths which return into themselves. The earliest, as also the latest, developed worlds - for the chain itself has grown by degrees - the furthest back, as also the furthest forward, are the most immaterial, the most ethereal of the whole series; and that this is in all ways in accordance with the fitness of things will appear from the reflection that the furthest forward of the worlds is not a region of finality, but the stepping-stone to the furthest back, as the month of December leads us back again to January. But it is not a climax of development from which the individual monad falls, as by a catastrophe, into the state from which he slowly began to ascend millions of years previously. From that which, for reasons which will soon appear, must be considered the highest world on the ascending arc of the circle, to that which must be regarded as the first on the descending arc, in one sense the lowest - i.e. in the order of development- there is no descent at all, but still ascent and progress. For the spiritual monad or entity, which has worked its way all round the cycle of evolution, at any one of the many stages of development into which the various existences around us may be grouped, begins its next cycle at the next higher stage, and is thus still accomplishing progress as it passes from world Z back again to world A. Many times does it circle, in this way, right round the system, but its passage round must not be thought of merely as a circular revolution in an orbit. In the scale of spiritual perfection it is constantly ascending. Thus, if we compare the system of worlds to a system of towers standing on a plain - towers each of many stories and symbolizing the scale of perfection - the spiritual monad performs a spiral progress round and round the series, passing through each tower, every time it comes round to it, at a higher level than before.

It is for want of realizing this idea that speculation, concerned with physical evolution, is so constantly finding itself stopped by dead walls. It is searching for its missing links in a world where it can never find them now, for they were but required for a temporary purpose, and have passed away. Man, says the Darwinian, was once an ape. Quite true; but the ape known to the Darwinian will never become a man - i.e. the *form* will not change from generation to generation till the tail disappears and the hands turn into feet, and so on. Ordinary science avows that, though changes of form can be detected in progress within the limits of species, the changes from species to species can only be inferred; and to account for these, it is content to assume great intervals of time and the extinction of the intermediate forms. There has been no doubt an extinction of the intermediate or earlier forms of all species (in the larger acceptation of the word) - i.e. of all kingdoms, mineral, vegetable, animal, man, &c. - but ordinary science can merely guess that to have been the fact without realizing the conditions which rendered it inevitable, and which forbid the renewed generation of the intermediate forms.

It is the spiral character of the progress accomplished by the life impulses that develop the various kingdoms of Nature, which accounts for the gaps now observed in the animated forms which people the earth. The thread of a screw, which is a uniform inclined plane in reality, looks like a succession of steps when examined only along one line parallel to its axis. The spiritual monads which are coming round the system on the animal level, pass on to other worlds when they have performed their turn of animal incarnation here. By the time they come again, they are ready for human incarnation, and there is no necessity now for the upward development of animal forms into human forms - these are already waiting for their spiritual tenants. But, if we go back far enough, we come to a period at which there were no human forms ready developed on the earth. When spiritual monads, traveling on the earliest or lowest human level, were thus beginning to come round, their onward pressure in a world at that time containing none but animal forms, provoked the improvement of the highest of these into the required form - the much-talked-of missing link.

In one way of looking at the matter, it may be contended that this explanation is identical with the inference of the Darwinian evolutionist in regard to the development and extinction of missing links. After all, it may be argued by a materialist, "we are not concerned to express an opinion as to the origin of the tendency in species to develop higher forms. We say that they do develop these higher forms by intermediate links, and that the intermediate links die out; and you say just the same thing." But there is a distinction between the two ideas for any one who can follow subtle distinctions. The natural process of evolution from the influence of local circumstances and sexual selection, must not be credited with producing intermediate forms, and this is why it is inevitable that the intermediate forms should be of a temporary nature and should die out. Otherwise, we should find the world stocked with missing links of all kinds, animal life creeping by plainly apparent degrees up to manhood, human forms mingling in indistinguishable confusion with those of animals. The impulse to the new evolution of higher forms is really given, as we have shown by rushes of spiritual monads coming round the cycle in a state fit for the inhabitation of new forms. These superior life impulses burst the chrysalis of the older form on the planet they invade, and throw off an efflorescence of something higher. The forms which have gone on merely repeating themselves for millenniums, start afresh into growth; with relative rapidity they rise through the intermediate into the higher forms, and then, as these in turn are multiplied with the vigour and rapidity of all new growths, they supply tenements of flesh for the spiritual entities coming round on that state or plane of existence, and for the intermediate forms there are no longer any tenants offering. Inevitably they become extinct.

Thus is evolution accomplished, as regards its essential impulse, by a *spiral progress* through the worlds. In the course of explaining this idea we have partly anticipated the declaration of another fact of first-rate importance as an aid to correct views of the world-system to which we belong. That is, that the tide of life, - the wave of existence, the spiritual impulse, call it by what name we please - passes on from planet to planet by rushes, or gushes, not by an even continuous flow. For the momentary purpose of illustrating the idea in hand, the process may be compared to the filling of a series of holes or tubs sunk in the ground, such as may sometimes be seen at the mouths of feeble springs, and connected with each other by little surface channels. The stream from the spring, as it flows, is gathered up entirely in the beginning by the first hole, or tub A, and it is only when this is quite full that the continued in-pouring of water from the spring causes that which it already contains to overflow into tub B. This in turn fills and overflows along the channel which leads to tub C, and so on. Now, though, of course, a clumsy analogy of this kind will not carry us very far, it precisely illustrates the evolution of life on a chain of worlds like that we are attached to, and, indeed the evolution of the worlds themselves. For the process which goes on does not involve the pre-existence of a chain of globes which Nature proceeds to stock with life; but it is one in which the evolution of each globe is the result of previous evolutions, and the consequence of certain impulses thrown off from its predecessor in the superabundance of their development. Now, it is necessary to deal with this characteristic of the process to be described, but directly we begin to deal with it we have to go back in imagination to a period in the development of our system very far antecedent to that which is specially our subject at present - the evolution of man. And manifestly, as soon as we begin talking of the beginnings of worlds, we are dealing with phenomena which can have had very little to do with *life*, as we understand the matter, and, therefore, it may be supposed, nothing to do with life impulses. But let us go back by degrees. Behind the human harvest of the life impulse, there lay the harvest of mere animal forms, as every one realizes; behind that, the harvest or growths of mere vegetable forms - for some of these undoubtedly preceded the appearance of the earliest animal life on the planet. Then, before the vegetable organizations, there were mineral organizations, - for even a mineral is a product of Nature, an evolution from something behind it, as every imaginable manifestation of Nature must be, until in the vast series of manifestations, the mind travels back to the unmanifested beginning of all things. On pure metaphysics of that sort we are not now engaged. It is enough to show that we may as reasonably - and that we must if we would talk about these matters at all - conceive a life impulse giving birth to mineral forms, as of the same sort of impulse concerned to raise a race of apes into a race of rudimentary men. Indeed, occult science travels back even further in its exhaustive analysis of evolution than the period at which minerals began to assume existence. In the process of developing worlds from fiery nebulae, Nature begins with something earlier than minerals - with the elemental forces that underlie the phenomena of Nature as visible now and perceptible to the senses of man. But that branch of the subject may be left alone for the present. Let us take up the process at the period when the first world of the series, - globe A let us call it, - is merely a congeries of mineral forms. Now it must be remembered that globe A has already been described as very much more ethereal, more predominated by spirit, as distinguished from matter, than the globe of what we at present are having personal experience, so that a large allowance must be made for that state of things when we ask the reader to think of it, at starting, as a mere congeries of mineral forms. Mineral forms may be mineral in the sense of not belonging to the higher forms of vegetable organism, and may yet be very immaterial as we think of matter, very ethereal, consisting of a very fine or subtle quality of matter, in which the other pole or characteristic of Nature, spirit, largely predominates. The minerals we are trying to portray are, as it were, the ghosts of minerals; by no means the highly-finished and beautiful, hard crystals which the mineralogical cabinets of this world supply. In these lower spirals of evolution with which we are now dealing, as with the higher ones, there is progress from world to world, and that is the great point at which we have been aiming. There is progress downwards, so to speak, in finish and materiality and consistency; and then, again, progress upward in spirituality as coupled with the finish which matter or materiality rendered possible in the first instance. It will be found that the process of evolution in its higher stages as regards man is carried on in exactly the same way. All through these studies, indeed, it will be found that one process of Nature typifies another, that the big is the repetition of the little on a larger scale.

It is manifest from what we have already said, and in order that the progress of organisms on globe A shall be accounted for, that the mineral kingdom will no more develop the vegetable kingdom on globe A until it receives an impulse from without, than the Earth was able to develop Man from the ape till it received an impulse from without. But it will be inconvenient at present to go back to a consideration of the impulses which operate on globe A in the beginning of the system's construction.

We have already, in order to be able to advance more comfortably from a far later period than that to which we have now receded, gone back so far that further recession would change the whole character of this explanation. We must stop somewhere, and for the present it will be best to take the life impulses behind globe A for granted. And having stopped there we may now treat the enormous period intervening between the mineral epoch on globe A and the man epoch, in a very cursory way, and so get back to the main problem before us. What has been already said facilitates a cursory treatment of the intervening evolution. The full development of the mineral epoch on globe A prepares the way for the vegetable development, as soon as this begins, the mineral life impulse overflows into globe B. Then when the vegetable development on globe A is complete and the animal development begins, the vegetable life impulse overflows to globe B, and the mineral impulse passes on to globe C. Then, finally, comes the human life impulse on globe A.

Now, it is necessary at this point to guard against one misconception that might arise. As just roughly described, the process might convey the idea that by the time the human impulse began on globe A, the mineral impulse was then beginning on globe D, and that beyond lay chaos. This is very far from being the case, for two reasons. Firstly, as already stated, there are processes of evolution which precede the mineral evolution, and thus a wave of evolution, indeed several waves of evolution, precede the mineral wave in its progress round the spheres. But over and above this, there is a fact to be stated which has such an influence on the course of events, that, when it is realized, it will be seen that the life impulse has passed several times completely round the whole chain of worlds before the commencement of the human impulse on globe A. This fact is as follows: Each kingdom of evolution, vegetable, animal, and so on, is divided into several spiral layers. The spiritual monads - the individual atoms of that immense life impulse of which so much as been said - do not fully complete their mineral existence on globe A, then complete it on globe B, and so on. They pass several times round the whole circle as minerals, and then again several times round as vegetables, and several times as animals. We purposely refrain for the present from going into figures, because it is more convenient to state the outline of the scheme in general terms first, but figures in reference to these processes of Nature have now been given to the world by the occult adepts (for the first time, we believe), and they shall be brought out in the course of this explanation very shortly, but, as we say, the outline is enough for any one to think of at first.

And now we have rudimentary man beginning his existence on globe A, in that world where all things are as the ghosts of the corresponding things in this world. He is beginning his long descent into matter. And the life impulse of each "round" overflows, and the races of man are established in different degrees of perfection on all the planets, on each in turn. But the rounds are more complicated in their design than this explanation would show, if it stopped short here. The process for each spiritual monad is not merely a passage from planet to planet. Within the limits of each planet, each time it arrives there, it has a complicated process of evolution to perform. It is many times incarnated in successive races of men before it passes onward, and it even has many incarnations in each great race. It will be found, when we get on further, that this fact throws a flood of light upon the actual condition of mankind, as we know it, accounting for those immense differences of intellect and morality, and even of welfare in its highest sense, which generally appear so painfully mysterious.

That which has a definite beginning generally has an end also. As we have shown that the evolutionary process under description began when certain impulses first commenced their operation, so it may be inferred that they are tending towards a final consummation, towards a goal and a conclusion. That is so, though the goal is still far off. Man, as we know him on this earth, is but half-way through the evolutionary process to which he owes his present development. He will be as much greater, before the destiny of our system is accomplished, than he is now, as he is now greater than the missing link. And that improvement will even be accomplished on this earth, while, in the other worlds of the ascending series, there are still loftier peaks of perfection to be scaled. It is utterly beyond the range of faculties untutored in the discernment of occult mysteries, to imagine the kind of life which man will thus ultimately lead before the zenith of the great cycle is attained. But there is enough to be done in filling up the details of the outline now presented to the reader, without attempting to forecast those which have to do with existences towards which evolution is reaching across the enormous abysses of the future.

Annotations

An expression occurs in the foregoing chapter which does not recommend itself to the somewhat fuller conceptions I have been able to form of the subject since this book was written. It is stated that "the spiritual monads - the individual atoms of that immense life impulse of which so much has been said - do not fully complete their mineral existence on globe A, then complete it on globe B, and so on. *They* pass several times round the whole circle as minerals, and then again several times round as vegetables, &c." Now it is intelligible to me that I was permitted to use this form of expression in the first instance because the main purpose in view was to elucidate the way in which the human entity was gradually evolved from processes of Nature going on in the first instance in lower kingdoms. But in truth at a later stage of the inquiry it becomes manifest that the vast process of which the evolution of humanity and all which that leads up to is the crowning act, the descent of spirit into matter, does not bring about a differentiation of individualities until a much later stage than is contemplated in the passage just quoted. In the mineral worlds on which the higher forms of plant and animal life have not yet been established, there is no such thing, as yet, as an individual spiritual monad, unless indeed by virtue of some inconceivable unity - inconceivable, but subject to treatment as a theory none the less - in the life impulses which are destined to give rise to the later chains of highly organized existence. Just as in a preceding note we assumed the unity of such a life impulse in the case of a perverted human Ego falling away as a whole from the current of evolution on which it was launched, so we may assume the same unity backwards to the earliest beginnings of the planetary chain. But this can be no more than a protective hypothesis, reserving us the right to investigate some mysteries later on that we need not go into at present. For a general appreciation of the subject it is better to regard the first infusion, as it were, of spirit into matter as provoking a homogeneous manifestations. The specific forms of the mineral kingdom, the crystals and differentiated rocks are but bubbles in the seething mass assuming partially individualized forms for a time, and rushing again into the general substance of the growing cosmos, not yet true individualities. Nor even in the vegetable kingdom does individuality set in. The vegetable establishes organic matter in physical manifestation, and prepares the way for the higher evolution of the animal kingdom. In this, for the first time, but only in the higher regions of this, is true individuality evoked. Therefore it is not till we begin in imagination to contemplate the passage of the great life impulse round the planetary chain on the level of animal incarnation, that it would be strictly justifiable to speak of the spiritual monads as traveling round the circle as a plurality, to which the word "they" would properly apply.

It is evidently not with the intention of encouraging any close study of evolution on the very grand scale with which we are dealing here, that the adept authors of the doctrine set forth in this volume, have opened the subject of the planetary chain. As far as humanity is concerned, the period during which this earth will be occupied by our race is more than long enough to absorb all our speculative energy. The magnitude of the evolutionary process to be accomplished during that period is more than enough to tax to the utmost the capacities of an ordinary imagination. But it is extremely advantageous for students of the occult doctrine to realize the plurality of worlds in our system once for all - their intimate relations with, their interdependence on each other - before concentrating attention on the evolution of this single planet. For in many respects the evolution of a single planet follows a routine, as it will be found directly, that bears an analogical resemblance to the routine affecting the entire series of planets to which it belongs. The older writings on occult science, of the obscurely worded order, sometimes refer to successive states of one world, as if successive worlds were meant, and vice versa. Confusion thus arises in the reader's mind, and according to the bent of his own inclination he clings to various interpretations of the misty language. The obscurity disappears when we realize that in the actual facts of Nature we have to recognize both courses of change. Each planet while inhabited by humanity, goes through metamorphoses of a highly important and impressive character, the effect of which may in each case be almost regarded as equivalent to the reconstitution of the world. But none the less, if the whole group of such changes is treated as a unity, does it form one of a higher series of changes. The several worlds of the chain are objective realities, and not symbols of change in one single, variable world. Further remarks on this head will fall into their place more naturally at the close of a later chapter.

# CHAPTER IV

## The World Periods

A striking illustration of the uniformities of Nature is brought out by the first glance at the occult doctrine in reference to the development of man on the earth. The outline of the design is the same as the outline of the more comprehensive design covering the whole chain of worlds. The inner details of this world, as regards its units of construction, are the same as the inner details of the larger organism of which this world itself is a unit. That is to say, the development of humanity on this earth is accomplished by means of successive waves of development which correspond to the successive worlds in the great planetary chain. The great tide of human life, be it remembered - for that has been already set forth - sweeps round the whole circle of worlds in successive waves. These primary growths of humanity may be conveniently spoken of as rounds. We must not forget that the individual units, constituting each round in turn, are identically the same as regards their higher principles, that is, that the individualities on the earth during round one come back again after completing their travels round the whole series of worlds and constitute round two, and so on. But the point to which special attention should be drawn here is that the individual unit, having arrived at any given planet of the series in the course of any given round, does not merely touch that planet and pass on to the next. Before passing on, he has to live through a series of races on that planet. And this fact suggests the outline of the fabric which will presently develop itself in the reader's mind, and exhibit that similarity of design on the part of one world as compared with the whole series, to which attention has already been drawn. As the complete scheme of Nature that we belong to is worked out by means of a series of rounds sweeping through all the worlds, so the development of humanity on each world is worked out by a series of races developed within the limits of each world in turn.

It is time now to make the working of this law clearer by coming to the actual figures which have to do with the evolution of our doctrine. It would have been premature to begin with them, but as soon as the idea of a system of worlds in a chain, and of life evolution on each through a series of rebirths, is satisfactorily grasped, the further examination of the laws at work will be greatly facilitated by precise reference to the actual number of worlds and the actual number of rounds and races required to accomplish the whole purpose of the system. For the whole duration of the system is as certainly limited in time, be it remembered, as the life of a single man. Probably not limited to any definite number of years set irrevocably from the commencement, but that which has a beginning progresses onward towards an end. The life of a man, leaving accidents quite out of the account, is a terminable period, and the life of a world system leads up to a final consummation. The vast periods of time, concerned in the life of a world system, dazzle the imagination as a rule, but still they are measurable; they are divisible into sub-periods of various kinds, and these have a definite number.

By what prophetic instinct Shakespeare pitched upon seven as the number which suited his fantastic classification of the ages of man, is a question with which we need not be much concerned; but certain it is that he could not have made a more felicitous choice. In periods of sevens the evolution of the races of man may be traced, and the actual number of the objective worlds which constitute our system, and of which the earth is one, is seven also. Remember, the occult scientists know this as a fact, just as the physical scientists know for a fact that the spectrum consists of seven colours, and the musical scale of seven tones. There are seven kingdoms of Nature, not three, as modern science has imperfectly classified them. Man belongs to a kingdom distinctly separate from that of the animals, including beings in a higher state of organization than that which manhood has familiarized us with as yet; and below the mineral kingdom there are three others, which science in the West knows nothing about; but this branch of the subject may be set aside for the present. It is mentioned merely to show the regular operation of the septenary law in Nature.

Man - returning to the kingdom we are most interested in - is evolved in a series of rounds (progressions round the series of worlds), and seven of these rounds have to be accomplished before the destinies of our system are worked out. The round which is at present going on is the fourth. There are considerations of the utmost possible interest connected with precise knowledge on these points, because each round is, as it were, specially allotted to the predominance of one of the seven principles in man, and in the regular order of their upward gradation.

An individual unit, arriving on a planet for the first time in the course of a round, has to work through seven races on that planet before he passes on to the next, and each of those races occupies the earth for a long time. Our old-fashioned speculations about time and eternity, suggested by the misty religious systems of the West, have brought on a curious habit of mind in connection with problems bearing on the actual duration of such periods. We can talk glibly of eternity, and, going to the other end of the scale, we are not shocked by a few thousand years, but directly years are numbered with precision in groups which lie in intervening regions of thought, illogical Western theologians are apt to regard such numbering as nonsense. Now, we at present living on this earth - the great bulk of humanity, that is to say, for there are exceptional cases to be considered later - are now going through the fifth race of our present fourth round. And yet the evolution of that fifth race began about a million of years ago. Will the reader, in consideration of the fact that the present cosmogony does not profess to work with eternity, nerve himself to deal with estimates that do concern themselves with millions of years, and even count such millions by considerable numbers?

Each race of the seven which go to make up a round - i.e. which are evolved on the earth in succession during its occupation by the great wave of humanity passing round the planetary chain - is itself subject to subdivision. Were this not the case, the active existences of each human unit would be indeed few and far between. Within the limits of each race there are seven subdivisional races, and again within the limits of each subdivision there are seven branch races. Through all these races, roughly speaking, each individual human unit must pass during his stay on earth, each time he arrives there, on a round of progress through the planetary system. On reflection, this necessity should not appal the mind so much as a hypothesis which would provide for fewer incarnations. For, however many lives each individual unit may pass through whole on earth during a round, be their numbers few or many, he cannot pass on until the time comes for the round wave to sweep forward. Even by the calculation already foreshadowed, it will be seen that the time spent by each individual unit in physical life can only be a small fraction of the whole time he has to get through between his arrival on earth and his departure for the next planet. The larger part of the time - as we reckon duration of time - is obviously, therefore, spent in those subjective conditions of existence which belong to the "World of Effects," or spiritual earth attached to the physical earth, on which our objective existence is passed.

The nature of existence on the spiritual earth must be considered *pari passu* with the nature of that passed on the physical earth, and dealt with in the above enumeration of race incarnations. We must never forget that between each physical existence the individual unit passes through a period of existence in the corresponding spiritual world. And it is because the conditions of that existence are defined by the use that has been made of the opportunities in the next, preceding physical existence, that the spiritual earth is often spoken of in occult writing as the world of effects. The earth itself is its corresponding world of causes.

That which passes naturally into the world of effects after an incarnation in the world of causes is the individual unit or spiritual monad; but the personality just dissolved passes there with it, to an extent dependent on the qualifications of such personality - on the use, that is to say, which the person in question has made of his opportunities in life. The period to be spent in the world of effects - enormously longer in each case than the life which has paved the way for existence there - corresponds to the "hereafter" or heaven of ordinary theology. The narrow purview of ordinary religious conceptions deals merely with one spiritual life and its consequences in the life to come. Theology conceives that the entity concerned had its beginning in this physical life, and that the ensuing spiritual life will never stop. And this pair of existences which is shown by the elements of occult science, that we are now unfolding, to constitute a part only of the entity's experience during its connection with a branch race which is one of seven belonging to a subdivisional race, itself one of seven belonging to a main race, itself one of seven belonging to the occupation of earth by one of the seven round-waves of humanity which have each to occupy it in turn before its functions in Nature are concluded - this microscopic molecule of the whole structure is what common theology treats as *more* than the whole, for it is supposed to cover eternity.

The reader must here be warned against one conclusion to which the above explanations - perfectly accurate as far as they go, but not yet covering the whole ground - might lead him. He will not get at the exact number of lives an individual entity has to lead on the earth in the course of its occupation by one round, if he merely raises seven to its third power. If one existence only were passed in each branch race the total number would obviously be 343, but each life descends at least twice into objectivity in the same branch - each monad, in other words, incarnates twice in each branch race. Again, there is a curious cyclic law which operates to augment the total number of incarnations beyond 686. Each subdivisional race has a certain extra vitality at its climax, which leads it to throw off an additional offshoot race at that point in its progress, and again another offshoot race is developed at the end of the subdivisional race by its dying momentum, so to speak. Through these races the whole tide of human life passes, and the result is that the actual normal number of incarnations for each monad is not far short of 800. Within relatively narrow limits it is a variable number, but the bearings of that fact may be considered later on.

The methodical law which carries each and every individual human entity through the vast evolutionary process thus sketched out, is in no way incompatible with that liability to fall away into abnormal destinies or ultimate annihilation which menaces the *personal* entities of people who cultivate very ignoble affinities. The distribution of the seven principles at death shows that clearly enough, but viewed in the light of these further explanations about evolution, the situation may be better realized. The permanent entity is that which lives through the whole series of lives not only through the races belonging to the present round-wave on earth, but also through those of other round-waves and other worlds. Broadly speaking, it may, in due time, though at some inconceivably distant future, as measured in years, recover a recollection of all those lives, which will seem as days in the past to us. But the astral dross, cast off at each passage into the world of effects, has a more or less independent existence of its own, quite separate from that of the spiritual entity from which it has just been disunited.

The natural history of this astral remnant is a problem of much interest and importance; but a methodical continuation of the whole subject will require us in the first instance to endeavour to realize the destiny of the higher and more durable spiritual Ego, and before going into that inquiry there is a good deal more to be said about the development of the objective races.

Esoteric science, though interesting itself mainly with matters generally regarded as appertaining to religion, would not be the complete comprehensive and trustworthy system that it is, if it failed to bring all the facts of earth life into harmony with its doctrines. It would have been little able to search out and ascertain the manner in which the human race has evolved through eons of time and series of planets, if it had not been in a position to ascertain also as the smaller inquiry is included in the greater, the manner in which the wave of humanity with which we are now concerned has been developed on this earth. The faculties, in short, which enable adepts to read the mysteries of other worlds, and of other states of existence, are in no way unequal to the task of travelling back along the life-current of this globe. It follows that while the brief record of a few thousand years is all that our so-called universal history can deal with, the earth history, which forms a department of esoteric knowledge, goes back to the incidents of the fourth race, which preceded ours, and to those of the third race, which preceded that. It goes back still further indeed, but the second and first races did not develop anything that could be called civilization, and of them therefore there is less to be said than of their successors. The third and fourth did - strange as it may seem to some modern readers to contemplate the notion of civilisation on the earth several millions of years ago.

Where are its traces? they will ask. How could the civilization with which Europe has now endowed mankind, pass away so completely that any future inhabitants of the earth could ever be ignorant that it once existed? How then can we conceive the idea that any similar civilisation can have vanished, leaving no records for us?

The answer lies in the regular routine of planetary life, which goes on *pari passu* with the life of its inhabitants. The periods of the great root races are divided from each other by great convulsions of Nature, and by great geological changes. Europe was not in existence as a continent at the time the fourth race flourished. The continent on which the fourth race lived was not in existence at the time the third race flourished. and neither of the continents which were the great vortices of the civilizations of these two races are in existence now. Seven great continental cataclysms occur during the occupation of the earth by the human life-wave for one round-period. Each race is cut off in this way at its appointed time, some survivors remaining in parts of the world, not the proper home of their race; but these, invariably in such cases, exhibiting a tendency to decay, and relapsing into barbarism with more or less rapidity.

The proper home of the fourth race, which directly preceded our own, was that continent of which some memory has been preserved even in exoteric literature - the lost Atlantis. But the great island, the destruction of which is spoken of by Plato, was really but the last remnant of the continent. "In the Eocene age," I am told, "even in its very first part, the great cycle of the fourth race men, the Atlanteans, had already reached its highest point, and the great continent, the father of nearly all the present continents, showed the first symptoms of sinking

- a process that occupied it down to 11,446 years ago, when its last island, that, translating its vernacular name, we may call with propriety Poseidonis, went down with a crash.

"Lemuria" (a former continent stretching southwards from India across what is now the Indian Ocean, but connected with Atlantis, for Africa was not then in existence) "should no more be confounded with the Atlantis continent than Europe with America. Both sank and were drowned, with their high civilizations and 'gods;' yet between the two catastrophes a period of about 700,000 years elapsed, Lemuria flourishing and ending her career just about that lapse of time before the early part of the Eocene age, since its race was the third. Behold the relics of that once great nation in some of the flat-headed aborigines of your Australia."

It is a mistake on the part of a recent writer on Atlantis to people India and Egypt with the colonies of that continent, but of that more anon.

"Why should not your geologists," asks my revered Mahatma teacher, "bear in mind that under the continents explored and fathomed by them, in the bowels of which they have found the Eocene age, and forced it to deliver them its secrets, there may be hidden deep in the fathomless, or rather unfathomed ocean beds, other and far older continents whose strata have never been geologically explored; and that they may some day upset entirely their present theories? Why not admit that our present continents have, like Lemuria and Atlantis, been several times already submerged, and had the time to reappear again, and bear their new groups of mankind and civilization; and that at the first great geological upheaval at the next cataclysm, in the series of periodical cataclysms that occur from the beginning to the end of every round, our already autopsized continents will go down, and the Lemurias and Atlantises come up again?

"Of course the fourth race had its periods of the highest civilization." (The letter from which I am now quoting was written in answer to a series of questions I put.) "Greek, and Roman, and even Egyptian civilizations are nothing compared to the civilizations that began with the third race. Those of the second race were not savages, but they could not be called civilized.

"Greeks and Romans were small sub-races, and Egyptians part and parcel of our own Caucasian stock. Look at the latter, and at India. Having reached the highest civilization, and, what is more, *learning*, both went down; Egypt, as a distinct sub-race, disappearing entirely (her Copts are but a hybrid remnant); India, as one of the first and most powerful offshoots of the mother race, and composed of a number of sub-races, lasting to these times, and struggling to take once more her place in history some day. That history catches but a few stray, hazy glimpses of Egypt some 12,000 years back, when, having already reached the apex of its cycle thousands of years before, the latter had begun to go down.

"The Chaldees were at the apex of their occult fame before what you term the Bronze Age. We hold - but then what warrant can you give the world that we are right? - that far greater civilizations than our own have risen and decayed. It is not enough to say, as some of your modern writers do, that an extinct civilization existed before Rome and Athens were founded. We affirm that a series of civilizations existed before as well as after the glacial period, that they existed upon various points of the globe, reached the apex of glory, and died. Every trace and memory had been lost of the Assyrian and Phoenician civilizations, until discoveries began to be made a few years ago. And now they open a new, though not by far one of the earliest pages in the history of mankind. And yet how far back to those civilizations go in comparison with the oldest, and even then history is slow to accept. Archaeology has sufficiently demonstrated that the memory of man runs back vastly further than history has been willing to accept, and the sacred records of once mighty nations, preserved by their heirs, are still more worthy of trust. We speak of civilizations of the ante-glacial period, and not only in the minds of the vulgar and the profane, but even in the opinion of the highly-learned geologist, the claim sounds preposterous. What would you say then to our affirmation that the Chinese - I now speak of the inland, the true Chinamen, not of the hybrid mixture between the fourth and fifth races now occupying the throne - the aborigines who belong in their unallied nationality wholly to the highest and last branch of the fourth race, reached their highest civilization when the fifth had hardly appeared in Asia. When was it? Calculate. The group of islands discovered by Nordenskiold of the Vega was found strewn with fossils of horses, sheep, oxen, &c., among gigantic bones of elephants, mammoths, rhinoceroses, and other monsters belonging to periods when man, says your science, had not yet made his appearance on earth. How came horses and sheep to be found in company with the huge antediluvians?

"The region now locked in the fetters of eternal winter, uninhabited by man - that most fragile of animals - will very soon be proved to have had not only a tropical climate, something your science knows and does not dispute, but having been likewise the seat of one of the most ancient civilizations of the fourth race, whose highest relics we now find in the degenerate Chinaman, and whose lowest are hopelessly (for the profane scientist) intermixed with the remnants of the third. I told you before that the highest people now on earth (spiritually) belong to the first sub-race of the fifth root race, and those are the Aryan Asiatics the highest race (physical intellectuality) is the last sub-race of the fifth - yourselves, the white conquerors. The majority of mankind belongs to the seventh sub-race of the fourth root race - the above-mentioned Chinamen and their offshoots and branchlets (Malayans, Mongolians, Tibetans, Javanese, &c., &c.) - with remnants of other sub-races of the fourth and the seventh sub-race of the third race. All these fallen, degraded semblances of humanity are the direct lineal descendants of highly civilized nations, neither the names nor memory of which have survived, except in such books as 'Populvuh,' the sacred book of the Guatemalans, and a few others unknown to science."

I had inquired was there any way of accounting for what seems the curious rush of human progress within the last two thousand years as compared with the relatively stagnant condition of the fourth-round people up to the beginning of modern progress. This question it was that elicited the explanations quoted above, and also the following remarks in regard to the recent "rush of human progress."

"The latter end of a very important cycle. Each round, each race, as every sub-race, has its great and its smaller cycles on every planet that mankind passes through. Our fourth-round humanity has its one great cycle, and so have its races and sub-races. 'The curious rush' is due to the double effect of the former - the beginning of its downward course - and of the latter (the small cycle of your sub-race) running on to its apex. Remember, you belong to the fifth race, yet you are but a western sub-race. Notwithstanding your efforts, what you call civilization is confined only to the latter and its offshoots in America. Radiating around, its deceptive light may seem to throw its rays on a greater distance than it does in reality. There is no rush in China, and of Japan you make but a caricature.

"A student of occultism ought not to speak of the stagnant condition of the fourth-round people, since history knows next to nothing of that condition, 'up to the beginning of modern progress,' of other nations but the Western. What do you know of America, for instance, before the invasion of that country by the Spaniards? Less than two centuries prior to the arrival of Cortez there was great a rush towards progress among the sub-races of Peru and Mexico as there is now in Europe and the United States. Their subrace ended in nearly total annihilation through causes generated by itself. We may speak only of the 'stagnant' condition into which, following the law of development, growth, maturity and decline every race and sub-race falls during the transition periods. It is that latter condition your universal history is acquainted with, while it remains superbly ignorant of the condition even, India was in some ten centuries back. Your sub-races are now running toward the apex of their respective cycles, and that history goes no further back that the periods of decline of a few other sub-races belonging most of them to the preceding fourth race."

I had asked to what epoch Atlantis belonged, and whether the cataclysm by which it was destroyed came in an appointed place in the progress of evolution, corresponding for the development of races to the obscuration of planets. The answer was: -

"To the Miocene times. Everything comes in its appointed time and place in the evolution of rounds, otherwise it would be impossible for the best seer to calculate the exact hour and year when such cataclysms great and small have to occur. All an adept could do would be to predict an approximate time, whereas now events that result in great geological changes may be predicted with as mathematical a certainty as eclipses and other revolutions in space. The sinking of Atlantis (the group of continents and isles) began during the Miocene period - as certain of your continents are now observed to be gradually sinking - and it culminated first in the final disappearance of the largest continent, an event coincident with the elevation of the Alps, and second, with that of the last of the fair islands mentioned by Plato. The Egyptian priests of Sais told his ancestor, Solon that Atlantis (i.e. the only remaining large island) had perished 9000 years before their time. This was not a fancy date, since they had for millenniums preserved most carefully their records. But then, as I say, they spoke but of the Poseidonis, and would not reveal even to the great Greek legislator their secret chronology. As there are no geological reasons for doubting, but, on the contrary, a mass of evidence for accepting the tradition, science has finally accepted the existence of the great continent and archipelago, and thus vindicated the truth of one more 'fable.'

"The approach of every new obscuration is always signalled by cataclysms of either fire or water. But, apart from this, every root race has to be cut in two, so to say, by either one or the other. Thus, having reached the apex of its development and glory, the fourth race - the Atlanteans - were destroyed by water; you find now but their degenerate fallen remnants, whose sub-races, nevertheless, each of them, has its palmy days of glory and relative greatness. What they are now, you will be some day, the law of cycles being one and immutable. When your race, the fifth, will have reached its zenith of physical intellectuality, and developed its highest civilization (remember the difference we make between material and spiritual civilizations), unable to go any higher in its own cycle, its progress towards absolute evil will be arrested (as its predecessors, the Lemurians and the Atlanteans, the men of the third and fourth races, were arrested in their progress towards the same) by one of such cataclysmic changes, its great civilization destroyed, and all the sub-races of that race will be found going down their respective cycles, after a short period of glory and learning. See the remnants of the Atlanteans, the old Greeks and Romans (the modern belong to the fifth race). See how great and how short, how evanescent were their days of fame and glory. For they were but sub-races of the seven offshoots of the root race. [Branches of the subdivisions, according to the nomenclature I have adopted previously.] No mother race, any more than her sub-races and offshoots, is allowed by the one reigning law to trespass upon the prerogatives of the race or sub-race that will follow it; least of all to encroach upon the knowledge and powers in store for its successor."

The "progress towards absolute evil." arrested by the cataclysms of each race in turn, sets in with the acquisition, by means of ordinary intellectual research and scientific advancement, of those powers over Nature which accrue even now in adeptship from the premature development of higher faculties than those we ordinarily employ. I have spoken slightly of these powers in a preceding chapter, when endeavouring to describe our esoteric teachers; to describe them minutely would lead me into a long digression on occult phenomena. It is enough to say that they are such as cannot but be dangerous to society generally, and provocative of all manner of crimes which would utterly defy detection, if possessed by persons capable of regarding them as anything else but a profoundly sacred trust. Now some of these powers are simply the practical application of obscure forces of Nature, susceptible of discovery in the course of ordinary scientific progress. Such progress had been accomplished by the Atlanteans. The worldly men of science in that race had learned the secrets of the disintegration and reintegration of matter, which few but practical spiritualists as yet know to be possible, and of control over the elementals, by means of which that and other even more portentous phenomena can be produced. Such powers in the hands of persons willing to use them for merely selfish and unscrupulous ends must not only be productive of social disaster, but also for the persons who hold them, of progress in the direction of that evilly spiritual exaltation which is a far more terrible result than suffering and inconvenience in this world. Thus it is, when physical intellect, unguarded by elevated morality, runs over into the proper region of spiritual advancement, that the natural law provides for its violent repression. The contingency will be better understood when we come to deal with the general destinies towards which humanity is tending.

The principle under which the various races of man as they develop are controlled collectively by the cyclic law, however they may individually exercise the free will they unquestionably possess, is thus very plainly asserted. For people who have never regarded human affairs as covering more than the very short period with which history deals, the course of events will perhaps, as a rule, exhibit no cyclic character, but rather a chequered progress, hastened sometimes by great men and fortunate circumstances, sometimes retarded by war, bigotry, or intervals of intellectual sterility, but moving continually onwards in the long account, at one rate of speed or another. As the esoteric view of the matter, fortified by the wide range of observation which occult science is enabled to take, has an altogether opposite tendency, it seems worth while to conclude these explanations with an extract from a distinguished author, quite unconnected with the occult world, who nevertheless, from a close observation of the mere historical record, pronounces himself decisively in favour of the theory of cycles. In his *History of the Intellectual Development of Europe* Dr J W. Draper writes as follows: -

"We are, as we often say, the creatures of circumstances. In that expression there is a higher philosophy than might at first sight appear . . . .From this more accurate point of view we should therefore consider the course of these events, recognizing the principle that the affairs of men pass forward in a determinate way, expanding and unfolding themselves. And hence we see that the things of which we have spoken as though they were matters of choice, were in reality force upon their apparent authors by the necessity of the times. But in truth they should be considered as the presentation of a certain phase of life which nations in their onward course sooner or later assume. To the individual, how well we know that a sober moderation of action, an appropriate gravity of demeanour, belong to the mature period of life, change from the wanton wilfulness of youth, which may be ushered in, or its beginning marked by, many accidental incidents; in one perhaps by domestic bereavements, in another by the loss of fortune, in a third by ill-health. We are correct enough in imputing to such trials the change of character; but we never deceive ourselves by supposing that it would have failed to take place had those incidents not occurred. There runs an irresistible destiny in the midst of all these vicissitudes . . . There are analogies between the life of a nation and that of an individual, who, though he may be in one respect the maker of his own fortunes, for happiness or for misery, for good or for evil, though he remains here or goes there, as his inclinations prompt, though he does this or abstains from that, as he chooses, is nevertheless held fast by an inexorable fate - a fate which brought him into the world involuntarily, as far as he was concerned, which presses him forward through a definite career, the stages of which are absolutely invariable - infancy, childhood, youth, maturity, old age, with all their characteristic actions and passions - and which removes him from the scene at the appointed time, in most cases against his will. So also it is with nations; the voluntary is only the outward semblance, covering, but hardly hiding, the predetermined. Over the events of life we may have control, but none whatsoever over the law of its progress. There is a geometry that applies to nations an equation of their curve of advance. That no mortal man can touch."

# CHAPTER V

# Devachan

It was not possible to approach a consideration of the states into which the higher human principles pass at death, without first indicating the general framework of the whole design worked out in the course of the evolution of man. That much of my task, however, having now been accomplished, we may pass on to consider the natural destinies of each human Ego in the interval which elapses between the close of one objective life and the commencement of another. At the commencement of another, the Karma of the previous objective life determines the state of life into which the individual shall be born. This doctrine of Karma is one of the most interesting features of Buddhist philosophy. There has been no secret about it at any time, though for want of a proper comprehension of elements in the philosophy, which have been strictly esoteric, it may sometimes have been misunderstood.

Karma is a collective expression applied to that complicated group of affinities for good and evil generated by a human being during life, and the character of which inheres in his fifth principle all through the interval which elapses between his death out of one objective life and his birth into the next. As stated sometimes, the doctrine seems to be one which exacts the notion of a superior spiritual authority summing up the acts of a man's life at its close, taking into consideration his good deeds and his bad, and giving judgment about him on the whole aspect of the case. But a comprehension of the way in which the human principles divide up at death, will afford a clue to the comprehension of the way in which Karma operates, and also of the great subject we may better take up first - the immediate spiritual condition of man after death.

At death the three lower principles - the body, its mere physical vitality, and its astral counterpart - are finally abandoned by that which really is the Man himself, and the four higher principles escape into that world immediately above our own; above our own, that is, in the order of spirituality - not above it at all, but in it and of it, as regards real locality - the astral plane or Kama Loca, according to a very familiar Sanskrit expression. Here a division takes place between the two duads, which the four higher principles include. The explanation already given concerning the imperfect extent to which the upper principles of man are as yet developed, will show that this estimation of the process, as in the nature of a mechanical separation of the principles, is a rough way of dealing with the matter. It must be modified in the reader's mind by the light of what has been already said. It may be otherwise described as a trial of the extent to which the fifth principle has been developed. Regarded in the light of the former idea, however, we must conceive the sixth and seventh principles, on the one hand, drawing the fifth, the human soul, in one direction, while the fourth draws it back earthwards in the other. Now, the fifth principle is a very complex entity, separable itself into superior and inferior elements. In the struggle which takes place between its late companion principles, its best, purest, most elevated and spiritual portions cling to the sixth, its lower instincts, impulses and recollections adhere to the fourth, and it is in a measure torn asunder. The lower remnant, associating itself with the fourth, floats off in the earth's atmosphere, while the best elements, those, be it understood, which really constitute the Ego of the late earthly personality, the individuality, the consciousness thereof, follow the sixth and seventh into a spiritual condition, the nature of which we are about to examine.

Rejecting the popular English name for this spiritual condition, as encrusted with too many misconceptions to be convenient, let us keep to the Oriental designation of that region or state into which the higher principles of human creatures pass at death. This is additionally desirable because, although the Devachan of Buddhist philosophy corresponds in some respects to the modern European idea of heaven, it differs from heaven in others which are even more important.

Firstly, however, in Devachan, that which survives is not merely the individual monad, which survives through all the changes of the whole evolutionary scheme, and flits from body to body, from planet to planet, and so forth - that which survives in Devachan is the man's own self-conscious personality, under some restrictions indeed, which we will come to directly, but still it is the same personality as regards its higher feelings, aspirations, affections, and even tastes, as it was on earth. Perhaps it would be better to say the essence of the late self-conscious personality.

It may be worth the reader's while to learn what Colonel H S. Olcott has to say in his *Buddhist Catechism* (14th thousand) of the intrinsic difference between "individuality" and "personality." Since he wrote not only under the approval of the High Priest of the Sripada and Galle, Sumangala, but also under the direct instruction of his Adept Guru, his words will have weight for the student of occultism. This is what he says in his appendix: -

"Upon reflection I have submitted 'personality' for 'individuality,' as written in the first edition. The successive appearances upon one or many earths, or 'descents into generation' of the tanhaically coherent parts (Skandas) of a certain being, are a succession of personalities. In each birth the personality differs from that of the previous or next succeeding birth. Karma, the *deus ex machina*, masks (or shall we say, reflects?) itself now in the personality of a sage, again as an artisan, and so on throughout the string of births. But though personalities ever shift, the one line of life along which they are strung like beads runs unbroken.

"It is ever that particular line, never any other. It is therefore individual, an individual vital undulation which began in Nirvana or the subjective side of Nature, as the light or heat undulation through aether began at its dynamic source;

is careering through the objective side of Nature, under the impulse of Karma and the creative direction of Tanha; and tends through many cyclic changes back to Nirvana. Mr Rhys Davids calls that which passes from personality to personality along the individual chain 'character' or 'doing.' Since 'character' is not a mere metaphysical abstraction, but the sum of one's mental qualities and moral propensities, would it not help to dispel what Mr Rhys Davids calls 'the desperate expedient of a mystery,' if we regarded the life undulation as individuality, and each of its series of natal manifestations as a separate personality?

"The denial of 'soul' by Buddha (see 'Sanyutto Nikaya,' the Sutta Pitaka) points to the prevalent delusive belief in an independent transmissible personality; and entity that could move from birth to birth unchanged, or go to a place or state where, as such perfect entity, it could eternally enjoy or suffer. And what he shows is that the 'I am I' consciousness is, as regards permanency, logically impossible, since its elementary constituents constantly change, and the 'I' of one birth differs from the 'I' of every other birth. But everything that I have found in Buddhism accords with the theory of a gradual evolution of the perfect man - viz. A Buddha through numberless natal experiences. And in the consciousness of that person who at the end of a given chain of beings attains Buddha-hood, or who succeeds in attaining the fourth stage of Dhyana, or mystic self-development, in any one of his births anterior to the final one, the scenes of all these serial births are perceptible. In the 'Jatakattahavannana,' so well translated by Mr Rhys Davids, an expression continually recurs which I think rather supports such an idea - viz. 'Then the blessed one *made manifest an occurrence hidden by change of birth,*' or 'that which had been hidden by, &c.' Early Buddhism, then, clearly held to a permanency of records in the Akasa, and the potential capacity of man to read the same when he has evolved to the stage of true individual enlightenment."

The purely sensual feelings and tastes of the late personality will drop off from it in Devachan, but it does not follow that nothing is preservable in that state, except feelings and thoughts having a direct reference to religion or spiritual philosophy. On the contrary, all the superior phases, even of sensuous emotion, find their appropriate sphere of development in Devachan. To suggest a whole range of ideas by means of one illustration, a soul in Devachan, if the soul of a man who was passionately devoted to music, would be continuously enraptured by the sensations music produces. The person whose happiness of the higher sort on earth had been entirely centered in the exercise of the affections will miss none in Devachan of those whom he or she loved. But, at once it will be asked, if some of these are not themselves fit for Devachan, how then? The answer is, that does not matter. For the person who loved them *they will be there.* It is not necessary to say much more to give a clue to the position. Devachan is a subjective state. It will seem, as real as the chairs and tables round us; and remember that, above all things, to the profound philosophy of occultism are the chairs and tables, and the whole objective scenery of the world, unreal and merely transitory delusions of sense. As real as the realities of this world to us, and even more so, will be the realities of Devachan to those who go into that state.

From this it ensues that the subjective *isolation* of Devachan, as it will perhaps be conceived at first, is not real isolation at all, as the word is understood on the physical plane of existence; it is companionship with all that the true soul craves for, whether persons, things, or knowledge. An a patient consideration of the place in Nature which Devachan occupies will show that this subjective isolation of each human unit is the only condition which renders possible anything which can be described as a felicitous spiritual existence after death for mankind at large, and Devachan is as much a purely and absolutely felicitous condition for all who attain it, as Avitchi is the reverse of it. There is no inequality or injustice in the system; Devachan is by no means the same thing for the good and the indifferent alike, but it is not a life of responsibility, and therefore there is no logical place for it for suffering, any more than in Avitchi there is any room for enjoyment or *repentance*. It is a life of *effects*, not of *causes*; a life of being paid your earnings, not of labouring for them. Therefore it is impossible to be during that life cognizant of what is going on on earth. Under the operation of such cognition there would be no true happiness possible in the state after death. A heaven which constituted a watch-tower, from which the occupants could still survey the miseries of the earth, would really be a place of acute mental suffering for its most sympathetic, unselfish, and meritorious inhabitants. If we invest them in imagination with such a very limited range of sympathy that they could be imagined as not caring about the spectacle of suffering after the few persons to whom they were immediately attached had died and joined them, still they would have a very unhappy period of waiting to go through before survivors reached the end of an often long and toilsome existence below. And even this hypothesis would be further vitiated by making heaven most painful for occupants who were most unselfish and sympathetic, whose reflected distress would thus continue on behalf of the afflicted race of mankind generally, even after their personal kindred had been rescued by the lapse of time. The only escape from this dilemma lies in the supposition that heaven is not yet opened for business, so to speak, and that all people who have ever lived from Adam downwards are still lying in a death-like trance, waiting for the resurrection at the end of the world. This hypothesis also has its embarrassments, but we are concerned at present with the scientific harmony of esoteric Buddhism, not with the theories of other creeds. Readers, however, who may grant that a purview of earthly life from heaven would render happiness in heaven impossible, may still doubt whether true happiness is possible in the state, as it may be objected, of monotonous isolation now described. The objection is merely raised from the point of view of an imagination that cannot escape from its present surroundings. To begin with, about monotony. No one will complain of having experienced monotony during the minute, or moment, or half-hour, as it may have been of the greatest happiness he may have enjoyed in life. Most people have had some happy moments, at all events, to look back to for the purpose of this comparison; and let us take even one such minute or moment, too short to be open to the least suspicion of monotony, and imagine its sensations immensely prolonged without any external events in progress to mark the lapse of time. There is no room, in such a condition of things, for the conception of weariness. The unalloyed, unchangeable sensation of intense happiness goes on and on, not for ever, because the causes which have produced it are not infinite themselves, but for very long periods of time, until the efficient impulse has exhausted itself.

Nor must it be supposed that there is, so to speak, no change of occupation for souls in Devachan - that any one moment of earthly sensation is selected for exclusive perpetuation. As a teacher of the highest authority on this subject writes: -

"There are two fields of causal manifestations - the objective and subjective. The grosser energies - those which operate in the denser condition of matter - manifest objectively in the next physical life, their outcome being the new personality of each birth marshaling within the grand cycle of the evolving individuality. It is but the moral and spiritual activities that find their sphere of effects in Devachan. And, thought and fancy being limitless, how can it be argued for one moment that there is anything like monotony in the state of Devachan? Few are the men whose lives were so utterly destitute of feeling, love, or of a more or less intense predilection for some one line of thought as to be made unfit for a proportionate period of Devachanic experience beyond their earthly life. So, for instance, while the vices, physical and sensual attractions, say, of a great philosopher, but a bad friend and a selfish man, may result in the birth of a new and still greater intellect, but at the same time a most miserable man, reaping the Karmic effects of all the causes produced by the 'old' being, and whose make-up was inevitable from the pre-ponderating proclivities of that being in the preceding birth, the intermedial period between the two physical births *cannot* be, in Nature's exquisitely well-adjusted laws, but a *hiatus* of unconsciousness. There can be no such dreary blank as kindly promised, or rather implied, by Christian Protestant theology, to the 'departed souls,' which, between death and 'resurrection,' have to hang on in space, in mental catalepsy, awaiting the 'Day of Judgment.' Causes produced by mental and spiritual energy being far greater and more important than those that are created by physical impulses, their effects have to be, for weal or woe, proportionately as great. Lives on this earth, or other earths, affording no proper field for such effects, and every labourer being entitled to his own harvest, they have to expand in either Devachan or Avitchi. [The lowest states of Devachan interchain with those of Avitchi.] Bacon for instance, whom a poet called

*'The brightest, wisest, meanest of mankind,'*

might reappear in his next incarnation as a greedy moneygetter, with extraordinary intellectual capacities. But, however great the latter, they would find no proper field in which that particular line of thought, pursued during his previous lifetime by the founder of modern philosophy, could reap all its dues. It would be but the astute lawyer, the corrupt Attorney-General, the ungrateful friend, and the dishonest Lord Chancellor, who might find, led on by his Karma, a congenial new soil in the *body* of the money-lender, and reappear as a new Shylock. But where would Bacon, the incomparable thinker, with whom philosophical inquiry upon the most profound problems of Nature was his 'first and last and only love,' where would this 'intellectual giant of his race,' once disrobed of his lower nature, go to? Have all the effects of that magnificent intellect to vanish and disappear? Certainly not. Thus his moral and spiritual qualities would also have to find a field in which their energies could expand themselves. Devachan is such a field. Hence all the great plans of moral reform, of intellectual research into abstract principles of Nature - all the divine, spiritual aspirations that had so filled the brightest part of his life would, in Devachan, come to fruition; and the abstract entity, known in the preceding birth as Francis Bacon, and that *may* be known in its subsequent re-incarnation as a despised usurer - that Bacon's own creation, his Frankenstein, the son of his Karma - shall in the meanwhile occupy itself in this inner world, also of its own preparation, in enjoying the effects of the grand beneficial spiritual causes sown in life. It would live a purely and spiritually conscious existence - a dream of realistic vividness - until Karma, being satisfied in that direction, and the ripple of force reaching the edge of its sub-cycle basin, the being should move into its next area of causes, either in this same world or another, according to his stage of progression . . . . Therefore, there *is* 'a change of occupation,' a continual change, in Devachan. For that dreamlife is but the fruition, the harvest-time, of those psychic seed-germs dropped from the tree of physical existence in our moments of dream and hope - fancy-glimpses of bliss and happiness, stifled in an ungrateful social soil, blooming in the rosy dawn of Devachan, and ripening under its ever-fructifying sky. If man had but one single moment of ideal experience, not even then could it be, as erroneously supposed, the indefinite prolongation of that 'single moment.' That one note, struck from the lyre of life, would form the key-note of the being's subjective state, and work out into numberless harmonic tones and semitones of psychic phantasmagoria. There, all unrealized hopes, aspirations, dreams, become fully realized, and the dreams of the objective become the realities of the subjective existence. And there, behind the curtain of Maya, its vaporous and deceptive appearances are perceived by the Initiate, who has learned the great secret how to penetrate thus deep into the Arcana of Being . . . ."

As physical existence has its cumulative intensity from infancy to prime, and its diminishing energy thenceforward to dotage and death, so the dream-life of Devachan is lived correspondentially. There is the first flutter of psychic life, the attainment of prime, the gradual exhaustion of force passing into conscious lethargy, semi-unconsciousness, oblivion and - not death, but birth! - birth into another personality and the resumption of action which daily begets new congeries of causes that must be worked out in another term of Devachan.

"It is not a reality then, it is a mere dream," objectors will urge; "the soul so bathed in a delusive sensation of enjoyment, which has no reality all the while, is being cheated by Nature, and must encounter a terrible shock when it wakes to its mistake." But, in the nature of things, it never does or can wake. The waking from Devachan is its next birth into objective life, and the draught of Lethe has then been taken. Nor as regards the isolation of each soul is there any consciousness of isolation whatever; nor is there ever possibly a parting from its chosen associates. Those associates are not in the nature of companions who may wish to go away, of friends who may tire of the friend that loves them, even if he or she does not tire of them. Love, the creating force, has placed their living image before the personal soul which craves for their presence, and that image will never fly away.

On this aspect of the subject I may again avail myself of the language of my teacher:-

"Objectors of that kind will be simply postulating an incongruity, an intercourse of entities in Devachan, which applies only to the mutual relationship of physical existence! Two sympathetic souls, both disembodied, will each work out its own Devachanic sensations, making the other a sharer in its subjective bliss. This will be as real to them, naturally, as though both were yet on this earth. Nevertheless, each is dissociated from the other as regards personal or corporeal association. While the latter is the only one of its kind that is recognized by our earth experience as an *actual* intercourse, for the Devachanee it would be not only something unreal, but could have no existence for it in any sense, not even as a delusion: a physical body or even a Mayavi-rupa remaining to its spiritual senses as invisible as it is itself to the physical senses of those who loved it best on earth. Thus even though one of the 'sharers' were alive and utterly unconscious of that intercourse in his waking state, still every dealing with him would be to the Devachanee an absolute *reality*. And what *actual* companionship could there ever be other than the purely idealistic one, as above described, between two *subjective* entities which are not even as material as that ethereal body-shadow - the Mayavi-rupa? To object to this on the ground that one is thus 'cheated by Nature,' and to call it ' a delusive sensation of enjoyment which has no reality,' is to show oneself utterly unfit to comprehend the conditions of life and being outside of our material existence. For how can the same distinction be made in Devachan - i.e. outside of the conditions of earth-life - between what we call a reality and a factitious or an artificial counterfeit of the same, in this, our world? The same principle cannot apply to the two sets of conditions. It is conceivable that what we call a reality in our embodied physical state will exist under the same conditions as an actuality for a disembodied entity? On earth, man is dual - in the sense of being a thing of matter and a thing of spirit; hence the natural distinction made by his mind - the analyst of his physical sensations and spiritual perceptions - between an actuality and a fiction; though, even in this life, the two groups of faculties are constantly equilibrating each other, each group when dominant seeing as fiction or delusion what the other believes to be most real. But in Devachan our Ego has ceased to be dualistic, in the above sense, and becomes a spiritual, mental entity. That which was a fiction, a dream in life, and which had its being but in the region of 'fancy,' becomes, under the new conditions of existence, the only possible *reality*. Thus, for us to postulate the possibility of any other reality for a Devachanee is to maintain an absurdity, a monstrous fallacy, an idea unphilosophical to the last degree. The actual is that which is acted or performed *de facto*: 'the reality of a thing is proved by its actuality.' And the suppositions and artificial having no possible existence in that Devachanic state, the logical sequence is that everything in it is actual and real. For, again, whether overshadowing the five principles during the life of the personality, or entirely separated from the grosser principles by the dissolution of the body - the sixth principle, or our 'Spiritual Soul,' has no substance - it is ever Arupa; nor is it confined to one place with a limited horizon of perceptions around it. Therefore, whether *in* or *out* of its mortal body it is ever distinct, and free from its limitations; and if we call its Devachanic experiences 'a cheating of Nature,' then we should never be allowed to call 'reality' any of those purely abstract feelings that belong entirely to, and are reflected and assimilated by, our *higher* soul - such, for instance, as an ideal perception of the beautiful, profound philanthropy, love, &c., as well as every other purely spiritual sensation that during life fills our inner being with either immense joy or pain."

We must remember that by the very nature of the system described there are infinite varieties of wellbeing in Devachan, suited to the infinite varieties of merit in mankind. If "the next world" really were the objective heaven which ordinary theology preaches, there would be endless injustice and inaccuracy in its operation. People, to begin with, would be either admitted or excluded, and the differences of favour shown to different guests within the all-favoured region would not sufficiently provide for differences of merit in this life. But the real heaven of our earth adjusts itself to the needs and merits of each new arrival with unfailing certainty. Not merely as regards the duration of the blissful state, which is determined by the causes engendered during objective life, but as regards the intensity and amplitude of the emotions which constitute that blissful state, the heaven of each person who attains the really existent heaven is precisely fitted to his capacity for enjoying it. It is the creation of his own aspirations and faculties. More than this it may be impossible for the uninitiated comprehension to realize. But this indication of its character is enough to show how perfectly it falls into its appointed place in the whole scheme of evolution.

"Devachan," to resume my direct quotations, "is, of course, a *state*, not a locality, as much as Avitchi, its antithesis (which please not to confound with *hell*). Esoteric Buddhist philosophy has three principal lokas so-called - namely, 1. *Kama loka*; 2. *Rupa loka*; and 3. *Arupa loka*; or in their literal translation and meaning - 1. world of desires or passions, of unsatisfied earthly cravings - the abode of 'Shells' and Victims, of Elementaries and Suicides; 2. the world of forms - i.e., of shadows more spiritual, having form and objectivity, but no substance; and 3. the *formless* world, or rather the world of no form, the incorporeal, since its denizens can have neither body, shape, nor colour for us mortals, and in the sense that we give to these terms. These are the three spheres of ascending spirituality in which the several groups of subjective and semi-subjective entities find their attractions. All but the suicides and the victims of premature violent deaths go, according to their attractions and powers, either into the Devachanic or the Avitchi state, which two states form the numberless subdivisions of Rupa and Arupa lokas - that is to say, that such states not only vary in degree, or in their presentation to the subject entity as regards form, colour, &c., but that there is an infinite scale of such states, in their progressive spirituality and intensity of feeling, from the lowest in the Rupa, up to the highest and the most exalted in the Arupa-loka. The student must bear in mind that *personality* is the synonym for limitation; and that the more selfish, the more contracted the person's ideas, the closer will he cling to the lower spheres of being, the longer loiter on the plane of selfish social intercourse."

Devachan being a condition of mere subjective enjoyment, the duration and intensity of which is determined by the merit and spirituality of the earth-life last past, there is no opportunity, while the soul inhabits it, for the punctual requital of evil deeds. But Nature does not content herself with either forgiving sins in a free and easy way, or damning sinners outright, like a lazy master too indolent, rather than too good-natured, to govern his household justly. The Karma of evil, be it great or small, is at certainly operative at the appointed time as the Karma of good. But the place of its operation is not Devachan, but either a new rebirth, or Avitchi - a state to be reached only in exceptional cases and by exceptional natures. In other words, while the common-place sinner will reap the fruits of his evil deeds in a following re-incarnation, the exceptional criminal, the aristocrat of sin, has Avitchi in prospect - that is to say, the condition of subjective spiritual misery which is the reverse side of Devachan.

"Avitchi is a state of the most *ideal spiritual* wickedness, something akin to the state of Lucifer, so superbly described by Milton. Not many, though, are there who can reach it, as the thoughtful reader will perceive. And if it is urged that since there is Devachan for nearly all, for the good, the bad, and the indifferent, the ends of harmony and equilibrium are frustrated, and the law of retribution and of impartial, implacable justice, hardly met and satisfied by such a comparative scarcity, if not absence of its antithesis, then the answer will show *that it is not so*. '*Evil* is the dark son of Earth (matter), and *Good* - the fair daughter of Heaven' (or Spirit), says the Chinese philosopher; hence the place of punishment for most of our sins is the earth - its birth-place and play-ground. There is more apparent and relative than actual evil even on earth, and it is not given to the *hoi polloi* to reach the fatal grandeur and eminence of a 'Satan' every day."

Generally the re-birth into objective existence is the event for which the Karma of evil patiently waits; and then it irresistibly asserts itself, not that the Karma of good exhausts itself in Devachan, leaving the unhappy monad to develop a new consciousness with no material beyond the evil deeds of its last personality. The re-birth will be qualified by the merit as well as the demerit of the previous life, but the Devachan existence is a rosy sleep - a peaceful night, with dreams more vivid than day, and imperishable for many centuries.

It will be seen that the Devachan state is only one of the conditions of existence which go to make up the whole spiritual or relatively spiritual complement of our earth life. Observers of spiritualistic phenomena would never have been perplexed, as they have been, if there were no other but the Devachan state to be dealt with. For once in Devachan there is very little opportunity for communication between a spirit, then wholly absorbed in its own sensations and practically oblivious of the earth left behind, and its former friends still living. Whether gone before or yet remaining on earth, those friends, if the bond of affection has been sufficiently strong, will be with the happy spirit still, to all intents and purposes for him, and as happy, blissful, innocent, as the disembodied dreamer himself. It is *possible*, however, for yet living persons to have visions of Devachan, though such visions are rare, and only one-sided, the entities in Devachan, sighted by the earthly clairvoyant, being quite unconscious themselves of undergoing such observation. The spirit of the clairvoyant ascends into the condition of Devachan in such rare visions, and thus becomes subject to the vivid delusions of that existence. It is under the impression that the spirits, with which it is in Devachanic bonds of sympathy, have come down to visit earth and itself, while the converse operation has really taken place. The clairvoyant's spirit has been raised towards those in Devachan. Thus many of the subjective spiritual communications - most of them when the sensitives are pure-minded - are real, though it is most difficult for the uninitiated medium to fix in his mind the true and correct pictures of what he sees and hears. In the same way some of the phenomena called psychography (though more rarely) are also real. The spirit of the sensitive, getting odylized, so to say, by the aura of the spirit in the Devachan, *becomes* for a few minutes that departed personality, and writes in the handwriting of the latter, in his language and in his thoughts, as they were during his lifetime. The two spirits become blended in one, and the preponderance of one over the other during such phenomena determines the preponderance of personality in the characteristic exhibited. Thus it may incidentally be observed, what is called *rapport*, is, in plain fact, an identity of molecular vibration between the astral part of the incarnate medium and the astral part of the disincarnate personality.

As already indicated, and as the common sense of the mater would show, there are great varieties of states in Devachan, and each personality drops into its befitting place there. Thence, consequently he emerges in his befitting place in the world of causes, this earth or another, as the case may be, when his time for rebirth comes. Coupled with survival of the affinities, comprehensively described as Karma, the affinities both for good and evil engendered by the previous life, this process will be seen to accomplish nothing less than an explanation of the problem which has always been regarded as so incomprehensible - the inequalities of life. The conditions on which we enter life are the consequences of the use we have made of our last set of conditions. They do not impede the development of fresh Karma, whatever they may be, for this will be generated by the use we make of *them* in turn. Nor is it to be supposed that every event of a current life which bestows joy or sorrow is old Karma bearing fruit. Many may be the immediate consequences of acts in the life to which they belong - ready-money transactions with Nature, so to speak, of which it may be hardly necessary to make any entry in her books. But the great inequalities of life, as regards the start in it which different human beings make, is a manifest consequence of old Karma, the infinite varieties of which always keep up a constant supply of recruits for all the manifold varieties of human condition.

It must not be supposed that the real Ego slips instantaneously at death from the earth life and its entanglements, into the Devachanic condition. When the division of, or purification of the fifth principle has been accomplished in Kama loca by the contending attractions of the fourth and sixth principles, the real Ego passes into a period of unconscious gestation. I have spoken already of the way in which the Devachanic life is in itself a process of growth, maturity, and decline; but the analogies of earth are even more closely preserved. There is a spiritual ante-natal state at the entrance to spiritual life, as there is a similar and equally unconscious physical state at the entrance to objective life. And this period, in different cases, may be of very different duration - from a few moments to immense periods of years. When a man dies, his soul or fifth principle becomes unconscious and loses all remembrance of things internal as wall as external. Whether his stay in Kama loca has to last but a few moments, hours, days, weeks, months or years, whether he dies a natural or a violent death, whether this occurs in youth or age, and whether the Ego has been good, bad, or indifferent, his consciousness leaves him as suddenly as the flame leaves a wick when it is blown out. When life has retired from the last particle of the brain matter, his perceptive faculties become extinct for ever, and his spiritual powers of cognition and volition become for the time being as extinct as the others. His Mayavi-rupa may be thrown into objectivity, as in the case of apparitions after death, but unless it is projected by a conscious or intense desire to see or appear to some one shooting through the dying brain, the apparition will be simply automatic. The revival of consciousness in Kama loca is obviously, from what has been said, a phenomenon that depends on the characteristic of the principles passing, unconsciously at the moment, out of the dying body. It may become tolerably complete under circumstances by no means to be desired, or it may be obliterated by a rapid passage into the gestation state leading to Devachan. This gestation state may be of very long duration in proportion to the Ego's spiritual stamina, and Devachan accounts for the remainder of the period between death and the next physical re-birth. The whole period is, of course, of very varying length in the case of different persons, but re-birth in less than fifteen hundred years is spoken of as almost impossible, while the stay in Devachan, which rewards a very rich Karma is sometimes said to extend to enormous periods.

Annotations

The comments I have to make on the doctrine embodied in the foregoing chapter will be postponed most conveniently to the end of the next, and offered in connection with those applying to the conditions of Kama loca.

# CHAPTER VI

## Kama Loca

The statements already made in reference to the destiny of the higher human principles at death will pave the way for a comprehension of the circumstances in which the inferior remnant of these principles finds itself, after the real Ego has passed either into the Devachanic state, or that unconscious intervening period of preparation therefore, which corresponds to physical gestation. The sphere in which such remnants remain for a time is known to occult science as Kama loca, the region of desire, not the region in which desire is developed to any abnormal degree of intensity, as compared with desire as it attaches to earth life, but the sphere in which that sensation of desire, which is a part of the earth life, is capable of surviving.

It will be obvious, from what has been said about Devachan, that a large part of the recollections which accumulate round the human Ego during life are incompatible in their nature with the pure subjective existence to which the real, durable, spiritual Ego passes; but they are not necessarily on that account extinguished or annihilated out of existence. They inhere in certain molecules of those finer (but not finest) principles, which escape from the body at death; and just as dissolution separates what is loosely called the soul from the body, so also it provokes a further separation between the constituent elements of the soul. So much of the fifth principle, or human soul, which is in its nature assimilable with, or has gravitated upward towards, the sixth principle, the spiritual soul, passes with the germ of that divine soul into the superior region, or state of Devachan, in which it separates itself almost completely from the attractions of the earth; quite completely, as far as its own spiritual course is concerned, though it still has certain affinities with the spiritual aspirations emanating from the earth, and may sometimes draw these towards itself. But the animal soul, or fourth, principle (the element of will and desire, as associated with objective existence), has no upward attraction, and no more passes away from the earth than the particles of the body consigned to the grave. It is not in the grave, however, that this fourth principle can be put away. It is not spiritual in its nature or affinities, but it is not physical in its nature. In its affinities it is physical, and hence the result. It remains within the actual physical local attraction of the earth - in the earth's atmosphere - or, since it is not the gases of the atmosphere that are specially to be considered in connection with the problem in hand, let us say, in Kama loca.

And with the fourth principle a large part (as regards most of mankind unfortunately, though a part very variable in its relative magnitude) inevitably remains. There are plenty of attributes which the ordinary composite human being exhibits, many ardent feelings, desires, and acts, floods of recollections, which, even if not concerned with a life as ardent perhaps as those which have to do with the higher aspirations, are nevertheless essentially belonging to the physical life, which take time to die. They remain behind in association with the fourth principle, which is altogether of the earthly perishable nature, and disperse or fade out, or are absorbed into the respective universal principles to which they belong just as the body is absorbed into the earth, in progress of time, and rapidly or slowly, in proportion to the tenacity of their substance. And where meanwhile is the consciousness of the individual who has died or dissolved? Assuredly in Devachan; but a difficulty presents itself to the mind untrained in occult science, from the fact that a semblance of consciousness inheres in the astral portion - the fourth principle, with a portion of the fifth - which remains behind in Kama loca. The individual consciousness, it is argued, cannot be in two places at once. But first of all, to a certain extent, it can. As may be perceived presently, it is a mistake to speak of consciousness, as we understand the feeling of life, attaching to the astral shell or remnant; but nevertheless a certain spurious manifestation of consciousness may be reawakened in the shell, without having any connection with the real consciousness all the while growing in strength and vitality in the spiritual sphere. There is no power on the part of the shell of taking in and assimilating new ideas and initiating courses of action on the basis of those new ideas. But there is in the shell a survival of volitional impulses imparted to it during life. The fourth principle is the instrument of volition, though not volition itself, and impulses imparted to it during life by the higher principles may run their course and produce results almost indistinguishable for careless observers from those which would ensue were the four higher principles really all united, as in life.

The fourth principle, is the vehicle during life of that essentially mortal consciousness which cannot suit itself to conditions of permanent existence; but the consciousness even of the lower principles *during life* is a very different thing from the vaporous, fleeting and uncertain consciousness which continues to inhere in them when that which really is the life, the over-shadowing of them, or their vitalization by the infusion of the spirit, has ceased, as far as they are concerned. Language cannot render all the facets of a many-sided idea intelligible at once, any more than a plain drawing can show all sides of a solid object. And at the first glance different drawings of the same object from different points of view may seem so unlike as to be unrecognizable as the same, but none the less, by the time they are put together in the mind, will their diversities be seen to harmonize. So with these subtle attributes of the invisible principles of man - no treatise can do more than discuss their different aspects separately. The various views suggested must mingle in the reader's mind before the complete conception corresponds to the realities of Nature.

In life the fourth principle is the seat of will and desire, but it is not will itself.

It must be alive, in union with the overshadowing spirit, or "one life," to be thus the agent of that very elevated function of life - will, in its sublime potency. As already mentioned, the Sanscrit names of the higher principles connote the idea that they are vehicles of the one life. Not that the one life is a separable molecular principle itself; it is the union of all - the influence of the spirit; but in truth the idea is too subtle for language, perhaps for intellect itself. Its manifestation in the present case, however, is apparent enough. Whatever the willing fourth principle may be when alive, it is no longer capable of active will when dead. But then, under certain abnormal conditions, it may partially recover life for a time; and this fact it is which explains many, though by no means all, of the phenomena of spiritualistic mediumship. The "elementary," be it remembered - as the astral shell has generally been called in former occult writings - is liable to be galvanized for a time in the mediumistic current into a state of consciousness and life, which may be suggested by the first condition of a person who, carried into a strange room in a state of insensibility during illness, wakes up feeble, confused in mind; gazing about with a blank feeling of bewilderment, taking in impressions, hearing words addressed to him, and answering vaguely. Such a state of consciousness is unassociated with the notions of past or future. It is an automatic consciousness, derived from the medium. A medium, be it remembered, is a person whose principles are loosely united and susceptible of being borrowed by other beings, or by floating principles, having an attraction for some of them or some part of them. Now what happens in the case of a shell drawn into the neighbourhood of a person so constituted? Suppose the person from whom the shell has been cast, died with some strong unsatisfied desire, not necessarily of an unholy sort, but connected entirely with the earth life, a desire, for example, to communicate some fact to a still living person. Certainly the shell does not go about in Kama loca with a persistent intelligent conscious purpose of communicating that fact; but, amongst others, the volitional impulse to do this has been infused into the fourth principle, and while the molecules of that principle remain in association, (and that may be for many years,) they only need a partial galvanization into life again, to become operative in the direction of the original impulse. Such a shell comes into contact with a medium (not so dissimilar in nature from the person who had died as to render a *rapport* impossible), and something from the fifth principle of the medium associates itself with the wandering fourth principle, and sets the original impulse to work. So much consciousness and so much intelligence as may be required to guide the fourth principle in the use of the immediate means of communication at hand - a slate and pencil, or a table to rap upon - is borrowed from the medium, and then the message given may be the message which the dead person originally ordered his fourth principle to give, so to speak, but which the shell has never till then had an opportunity of giving. It may be argued that the production of writing on a closed slate, or of raps on a table without the use of a knuckle or a stick, is itself a feat of a marvellous nature, bespeaking a knowledge on the part of the communicating intelligence of powers in Nature we in physical life know nothing about. But the shell is itself in the astral world; in the realm of such powers. A phenomenal manifestation is its natural mode of dealing. It is no more conscious of producing a wonderful result by the use of new powers acquired in a higher sphere of existence, than we are conscious of the forces by which in life the volitional impulse is communicable to nerves and muscles.

But, it may be objected, the "communicating intelligence" at a spiritual seance will constantly perform remarkable feats for no other than their own sake, to exhibit the power over natural forces which it possesses. The reader will please remember, however, that occult science is very far from saying that all the phenomena of spiritualism are traceable to one class of agents. Hitherto in this treatise little has been said of the "elementals," those semi-intelligent creatures of the astral light, who belong to a wholly different kingdom of Nature from ourselves. Nor is it possible at present to enlarge upon their attributes, for the simple and obvious reason that knowledge concerning the elementals, detailed knowledge on that subject, and in regard to the way they work, is scrupulously withheld by the adepts of occultism. To possess such knowledge is to wield power, and the whole motive of the great secrecy in which occult science is shrouded turns upon the danger of conferring powers upon people who have not, first of all, by undergoing the training of initiates, given moral guarantees of their trustworthiness. It is by command over the elementals that some of the greatest physical feats of adeptship are accomplished; and it is by the spontaneous playful acts of the elementals that the greatest physical phenomena of the seance room are brought about. So also with almost all Indian Fakirs and Yogis of the lower class who have power of producing phenomenal results. By some means, by a scrap of inherited occult teaching, most likely, they have come into possession of a morsel of occult science. They may not necessarily understand the action of the forces they employ, any more than an Indian servant in a telegraph office, taught how to mix the ingredients of the liquid used in a galvanic battery, understands the theory of electric science. He can perform the one trick he has been taught; and so with the inferior Yogi. He has got influence over certain elementals, and can work certain wonders.

Returning to a consideration of the ex-human shells in Kâma loca, it may be argued that their behaviour in spiritual seances is not covered by the theory that they have had some message to deliver from their late master, and have availed themselves of the mediumship present, to deliver it. Apart altogether from phenomena that may be put aside as elemental pranks, we sometimes encounter a continuity of intelligence on the part of the elementary or shell that bespeaks much more than the survival of impulses from the former life. Quite so; but with portions of the medium's fifth principle conveyed into it, the fourth principle is once more an instrument in the hands of a master. With a medium entranced so that the energies of the fifth principle are conveyed into the wandering shell to a very large extent, the result is that there is a very tolerable revival of consciousness in the shell for the time being, as regards the given moment. But what is the nature of such consciousness, after all? Nothing more, really, than a reflected light. Memory is one thing, and perceptive faculties quite another. A madman may remember very clearly some portions of his past life; yet he is unable to perceive anything in its true light, for the higher portion of his Manas, fifth, and Buddhi, sixth, principles, are paralysed in him and have left him. Could an animal - a dog, for instance - explain himself, he could prove that his memory, in direct relation to his canine personality, is as fresh as his master's; nevertheless, his memory and instinct cannot be called perceptive faculties.

Once that a shell is in the aura of a medium, he will perceive, clearly enough, whatever he can perceive through the borrowed principles of the medium, and through organs in magnetic sympathy therewith; but this will not carry him beyond the range of the perceptive faculties of the medium, or of some one else present in the circle. Hence the often rational and sometimes highly intelligent answers he may give, and hence, also, his invariably complete oblivion of all things unknown to that medium or circle, or not found in the lower recollections of his late personality, galvanized afresh by the influences under which he is placed. The shell of a highly intelligent, learned, but utterly unspiritual man, who died a natural death, will last longer than those of weaker temperament, and (the shadow of his own memory helping) he may deliver, through trance-speakers, orations of no contemptible kind. But these will never be found to relate to anything beyond the subjects he thought much and earnestly of during life, nor will any word ever fall from him indicating a real advance of knowledge.

It will easily be seen that a shell, drawn into the mediumistic current, and getting into *rapport* with the medium's fifth principle, is not by any means sure to be animated with a consciousness (even for what such consciousness are worth) identical with the personality of the dead person from whose higher principles it was shed. It is just as likely to reflect some quite different personality, caught from the suggestions of the medium's mind. In this personality it will perhaps remain and answer for a time; then some new current of thought thrown into the minds of the people present, will find its echo in the fleeting impressions of the elementary, and his sense of identity will begin to waver; for a little while it flickers over two or three conjectures, and ends by going out altogether for a time. The shell is once more sleeping in the astral light, and may be unconsciously wafted in a few moments to the other ends of the earth.

Besides the ordinary elementary or shell of the kind just described, Kâma loca is the abode of another class of astral entities, which must be taken into account if we desire to comprehend the various conditions under which human creatures may pass from this life to others. So far we have been examining the normal course of events, when people die in a natural manner. But an abnormal death will lead to abnormal consequences. Thus, in the case of persons committing suicide, and in that of persons killed by sudden accident, results ensue which differ widely from those following natural deaths. A thoughtful consideration of such cases must show, indeed, that in a world governed by rule and law, by affinities working out their regular effects in that deliberate way which Nature favours, the case of a person dying a sudden death at a time when all his principles are firmly united, and ready to hold together for twenty, forty, or sixty years, whatever the natural remainder of his life would be, must surely be something different from that of a person who, by natural processes of decay, finds himself, when the vital machine stops, readily separable into his various principles, each prepared to travel their separate ways. Nature, always fertile in analogies, at once illustrates the idea by showing us a ripe and an unripe fruit. From out of the first the inner stone will come away as cleanly and easily as a hand from a glove, while from the unripe fruit the stone can only be torn with difficulty, half the pulp clinging to its surface. Now, in the case of the sudden accidental death or of the suicide, the stone has to be torn from the unripe fruit. There is no question here about the moral blame which may attach to the act of suicide. Probably, in the majority' of cases, such moral blame does attach to it, but that is a question of Karma which will follow the person concerned into the next re-birth, like any other Karma, and has nothing to do with the immediate difficulty such person may find in getting himself thoroughly and wholesomely dead. This difficulty is manifestly just the same, whether a person kills himself, or is killed in the heroic discharge of duty, or dies the victim of an accident over which he has no control whatsoever.

As an ordinary rule, when a person dies, the long account of Karma naturally closes itself - that is to say, the complicated set of affinities which have been set up during life in the first durable principle, the fifth, is no longer susceptible of extension. The balance-sheet, so to speak, is made out afterwards, when the time comes for the next objective birth; or, in other words, the affinities long dormant in Devachan, by reason of the absence there of any scope for their action, assert themselves as soon as they come in contact once more with physical existence. But the fifth principle, in which these affinities are grown, cannot be separated, in the case of the person dying prematurely, from the earthly principle - the fourth. The elementary, therefore, which finds itself in Kâma loca, on its violent expulsion from the body is not a mere shell - it is the person himself, who was lately alive, *minus* nothing but the body. In the true sense of the word, he is not dead at all.

Certainly elementaries of this kind may communicate very effectually at spiritual seances at their own heavy cost; for they are unfortunately able, by reason of the completeness of their astral constitution, to go on generating Karma, to assuage their thirst for life at the unwholesome spring of mediumship. If they were of a very material sensual type in life, the enjoyments they will seek will be of a kind the indulgence of which in their disembodied state may readily be conceived even more prejudicial to their Karma than similar indulgences would have been in life. In such cases *facilis est descensus*. Cut off in the full flush of earthly passions which bind them to familiar scenes, they are enticed by the opportunity which mediums afford for the gratification of these vicariously. They become the incubi and succubi of mediaeval writing, demons of thirst and gluttony, provoking their victims to crime. A brief essay on this subject, which I wrote last year, and from which I have reproduced some of the sentences just given, appeared in the Theosophist, with a note, the authenticity of which I have reason to trust, and the tenor of which was as follows: -

"The variety of states after death is greater if possible than the variety of human lives upon this earth. The victims of accident do not generally become earth walkers, only those falling into the current of attraction who die full of some engrossing earthly passion, the *selfish*, who have never given a thought to the welfare of others. Overtaken by death in the consummation, whether real or imaginary, of some master passion of their lives, the desire remaining unsatisfied, even after a full realization, and they still craving for more, such personalities can never pass beyond the earth attraction to wait for the hour of deliverance in happy ignorance and full oblivion. Among the suicides, those to whom the above statement about provoking their victims to crime, &c., applies, are that class who commit the act, in consequence of a crime, to escape the penalty of human law or their own remorse. Natural law cannot be broken with impunity; the inexorable causal relation between action and result has its full sway only in the world of effects, the Kâma loca, and every case is met there by an adequate punishment, and in a thousand ways, that would require volumes even to describe them superficially."

Those who "wait for the hour of deliverance in happy ignorance and full oblivion" are of course such victims of accident as have already on earth engendered pure and elevated affinities, and after death are as much beyond the reach of temptation in the shape of mediumistic currents as they would have been inaccessible in life to common incitements to crime. Entities of another kind occasionally to be found in Kâma loca have yet to be considered. We have followed the higher principles of persons recently dead, observing the separation of the astral dross from the spirituality durable portion; that spirituality durable portion being either holy or Satanic in its nature, and provided for in Devachan or Avitchi accordingly. We have examined the nature of the elementary shell cast off and preserving for a time a deceptive resemblance to a true entity; we have paid attention also to the exceptional cases of real four-principled beings in Kâma loca who are the victims of accident or suicide. But what happens to a personality which has absolutely no atom of spirituality, no trace of spiritual affinity in its fifth principle, either of the good or bad sort? Clearly in such a case there is nothing for the sixth principle to attract to itself. Or, in other words, such a personality has already lost its sixth principle by the time death comes. But Kâma loca is no more a sphere of existence for such a personality than the subjective world; Kâma loca may be permanently inhabited by astral beings, by elementals, but can only be an antechamber to some other state for human beings.

In the case imagined, the surviving personality is promptly drawn into the current of its future destinies, and these have nothing to do with this earth's atmosphere or with Devachan, but with that "eighth sphere" of which occasional mention will be found in older occult writings. It will have been unintelligible to ordinary readers hitherto why it was called the "eighth" sphere, but since the explanation, now given out for the first time, of the sevenfold constitution of our planetary system, the meaning will be clear enough. The spheres of the cyclic process of evolution are seven in number, but there is an eighth in connection with our earth, our earth being, it will be remembered, the turning-point in the cyclic chain, and this eighth sphere is out of circuit, a *cul de sac*, and the bourne from which it may be truly said no traveller returns.

It will readily be guessed that the only sphere connected with our planetary chain, which is lower than our own in the scale, having spirit at the top and matter at the bottom, must itself be no less visible to the eye and to optical instruments than the earth itself, and as the duties which this sphere has to perform in our planetary system are immediately associated with this earth, there is not much mystery left now in the riddle of the eighth sphere, nor as to the place in the sky where it may be sought. The conditions of existence there, however, are topics on which the adepts are very reserved in their communications to uninitiated pupils, and concerning these I have for the present no further information to give.

One statement though is definitely made-viz., that such a total degradation of a personality as may suffice to draw it, after death, into the attraction of the eighth sphere, is of very rare occurrence. From the vast majority of lives there is something which the higher principles may draw to themselves, something to redeem the page of existence just passed from total destruction, and here it must be remembered that the recollections of life in Devachan, very vivid as they are, as far as they go, touch only those episodes in life that are productive of the elevated sort of happiness of which alone Devachan is qualified to take cognizance, whereas the life from which, for the time being, the cream is thus skimmed, may come to be remembered eventually in all its details quite fully. That complete remembrance is only achieved by the individual at the threshold of a far more exalted spiritual state than that which we are now concerned with; one which is attained far later on in the progress of vast cycles of evolution. Each one of the long series of lives that will have been passed through will then be, as it were, a page in a book to which the possessor can turn back at pleasure, even though many such pages will then seem to him most likely, very dull reading, and will not be frequently referred to. It is this revival eventually of recollection concerning all the long-forgotten personalities that is really meant by the doctrine of the Resurrection. But we have no time at present to stop and unravel the enigmas of symbolism as bearing upon the teachings at present under conveyance to the reader. It may be worth while to do this as a separate undertaking at a later period; but meanwhile, to revert to the narrative of how the facts stand, it may be explained that in the whole book of pages, when at last the "resurrection" has been accomplished, there will be no entirely infamous pages; for even if any given spiritual individuality has occasionally, during its passage through this world, been linked with personalities so deplorably and desperately degraded that they have passed completely into the attraction of the lower vortex, that spiritual individuality in such cases will have retained, in its own affinities, no trace or taint of them. Those pages will, as it were, have been cleanly torn out from the book. And, as at the end of the struggle, after crossing Kâma loca, the spiritual individuality will have passed into the unconscious gestation state from which, skipping the Devachan state, it will be directly (though not immediately in time) reborn into its next life of objective activity, all the self-consciousness connected with that existence will have passed into the lower world, there eventually to "perish everlastingly;" an expression of which, as of so many more, modern theology has proved a faithless custodian, making pure nonsense out of psycho-scientific facts.

Annotations

There is no part of the present volume which I now regard as in so much urgent need of amplification as the two chapters which have just been passed. The Kâma loca stage of existence, and that higher region or state of Devachan, to which it is but the antechamber, were, designedly I take it, left by our teachers in the first instance in partial obscurity, in order that the whole scheme of evolution might be the better understood. The spiritual state which immediately follows our present physical life, is a department of Nature, the study of which is almost unhealthily attractive for every one who once realizes that some contact with it - some processes of experiment with its conditions - are possible even during this life. Already we can to a certain extent discern the phenomena of that state of existence into which a human creature passes at the death of the body. The experience of spiritualism has supplied us with facts concerning it in very great abundance. These facts are but too highly suggestive of theories and inferences which seem to reach the ultimate limits of speculation, and nothing but the bracing mental discipline of esoteric study in its broadest aspect will protect any mind addressed to the consideration of these facts from conclusions which that study shows to be necessarily erroneous. For this reason, theosophical inquirers have nothing to regret as far as their own progress in spiritual science is at stake, in the circumstances which have hitherto induced them to be rather neglectful of the problems that have to do with the state of existence next following our own. It is impossible to exaggerate the intellectual advantages to be derived from studying the broad design of Nature throughout those vast realms of the future which only the perfect clairvoyance of the adepts can penetrate, before going into details regarding that spiritual foreground, which is partially accessible to less powerful vision, but liable, on a first acquaintance, to be mistaken for the whole expanse of the future.

The earlier processes, however, through which the soul passes at death, may be described at this date somewhat more fully than they are defined in the foregoing chapter. The nature of the struggle that takes place in Kâma loca between the upper and lower duads may now, I believe, be apprehended more clearly than at first. That struggle appears to be a very protracted and variegated process, and to constitute,- not as some of us may have conjectured at first, an automatic or unconscious assertion of affinities or forces quite ready to determine the future of the spiritual monad at the period of death, - but a phase of existence which may be, and in the vast majority of cases is more than likely to be, continued over a considerable series of years. And during this phase of existence it is quite possible for departed human entities to manifest themselves to still living persons through the agency of spiritual mediumship, in a way which may go far towards accounting for, if it does not altogether vindicate, the impressions that spiritualists derive from such communications.

But we must not conclude too hastily that the human soul going through the struggle or evolution of Kâma loca is in all respects what the first glance at the position, as thus defined, may seem to suggest. First of all, we must beware of too grossly materializing our conception of the struggle, by thinking of it as a mechanical separation of principles. There is a mechanical separation involved in the discard of lower principles when the consciousness of the Ego is firmly seated in the higher. Thus at death the body is mechanically discarded by the soul, which (in union, perhaps, with intermediate principles), may actually be seen by some clairvoyants of a high order to quit the tenement it needs no longer. And a very similar process may ultimately take place in Kâma loca itself, in regard to the matter of the astral principles. But postponing this consideration for a few moments, it is important to avoid supposing that the struggle of Kâma loca does itself constitute this ultimate division of principles, or second death upon the astral plane.

The struggle of Kâma loca is in fact the life of the entity in that phase of existence. As quite correctly stated in the text of the foregoing chapter, the evolution taking place during that phase of existence is not concerned with the responsible choice between good and evil which goes on during physical life. Kâma loca is a portion of the great world of effects, - not a sphere in which causes are generated (except under peculiar circumstances). The Kâma loca entity, therefore, is not truly master of his own acts; he is rather the sport of his own already established affinities. But these are all the while asserting themselves, or exhausting themselves, *by degrees*, and the Kâma loca entity has an existence of vivid consciousness of one sort or another the whole time. Now a moment's reflection will show that those affinities, which are gathering strength and asserting themselves, have to do with the *spiritual* aspirations of the life last experienced, while those which are exhausting themselves have to do with its *material* tastes, emotions, and proclivities. The Kâma loca entity, be it remembered, is on his way to Devachan, or, in other words, is growing into that state which is the Devachanic state, and the process of growth is accomplished by action and reaction, by ebb and flow, like almost every other in Nature, - by a species of oscillation between the conflicting attractions of matter and spirit. Thus the Ego advances towards Heaven, so to speak, or recedes towards earth, during his Kâma loca existence, and it is just this tendency to oscillate between the two poles of thought or condition, that brings him back occasionally within the sphere of the life he has just quitted.

It is not by any means at once that his ardent sympathies with that life are dissipated. His sympathies with the higher aspects of that life, be it remembered, are not even on their way to dissipation. For instance, in what is here referred to as earthly affinity, we need not include the exercise of affection, which is a function of Devachanic existence in a pre-eminent degree. But perhaps even in regard to his affections there may be earthly and spiritual aspects of these, and the contemplation of them, with the circumstances and surroundings of the earth-life, may often have to do with the recession towards earthlife of the Kâma loca entity referred to above.

Of course it will be apparent at once that the intercourse which the practice of spiritualism sets up between the Kâma loca entities as here in view, and the friends they have left on earth, must go on during those periods of the soul's existence in which earth memories engage its attention; and there are two considerations of a very important nature which arise out of this reflection.

1st. While its attention is thus directed, it is turned away from the spiritual progress on which it is engaged during its oscillations in the other direction. It may fairly well remember, and in conversation refer to, the spiritual aspirations of the life on earth, but its new spiritual experiences appear to be of an order that cannot be translated back into terms of the ordinary physical intellect, and, besides that, to be not within the command of the faculties which are in operation in the soul during its occupation with old-earth memories. The position might be roughly symbolized, but only to a very imperfect extent, by the case of a poor emigrant, whom we may imagine prospering in his new country, getting educated there, concerning himself with its public affairs and discoveries, philanthropy, and so on. He may keep up an interchange of letters with his relations at home, but he will find it difficult to keep them au courant with all that has come to be occupying his thoughts. The illustration will only fully apply to our present purpose, however, if we think of the emigrant as subject to a psychological law which draws a veil over his understanding when he sits down to write to his former friends, and restores him during that time to his former mental condition. He would then be less and less able to write about the old topics as time went on, for they would not only be below the level of those to the consideration of which his real mental activities had risen, but would to a great extent have faded from his memory. His letters would be a source of surprise to their recipients, who would say to themselves that it was certainly so-and-so who was writing, but that he had grown very dull and stupid compared to what he used to be before he went abroad.

2ndly. It must be borne in mind that a very well-known law of physiology, according to which faculties are invigorated by use and atrophied by neglect, applies on the astral as well as on the physical plane. The soul in Kâma loca, which acquires the habit of fixing its attention on the memories of the life it has quitted, will strengthen and harden those tendencies which are at war with its higher impulses. The more frequently it is appealed to by the affection of friends still in the body to avail itself of the opportunities furnished by mediumship for manifesting its existence on the physical plane, the more vehement will be the impulses which draw it back to physical life, and the more serious the retardation of its spiritual progress. This consideration appears to involve the most influential motive which leads the representatives of Theosophical teaching to discountenance and disapprove of all attempts to hold communication with departed souls by means of the spiritual seance. The more such communications are genuine the more detrimental they are to the inhabitants of Kâma loca concerned with them. In the present state of our knowledge it is difficult to determine with confidence the extent to which the Kâma loca entities are thus injured. And we may be tempted to believe that in some cases the great satisfaction derived by the living persons who communicate, may outweigh the injury so inflicted on the departed soul. This satisfaction, however, will only be keen in proportion to the failure of the still living friend to realize the circumstances under which the communication takes place. At first, it is true, very shortly after death, the still vivid and complete memories of earth-life may enable the Kâma loca entity to manifest himself as a personage very fairly like his deceased self, but from the moment of death the change in the direction of his evolution sets in. He will, as manifesting on the physical plane, betray no fresh fermentation of thought in his mind. He will never, in that manifestation, be any wiser, or higher in the scale of Nature, than he was when he died; on the contrary, he must become less and less intelligent, and apparently less instructed than formerly, as time goes on. He will never do himself justice in communication with the friends left behind, and his failure in this respect will grow more and more painful by degrees.

Yet another consideration operates to throw a very doubtful light on the wisdom or propriety of gratifying a desire for intercourse with deceased friends. We may say, never mind the gradually fading interest of the friend who has gone before, in the earth left behind; while there is anything of his or her old self left to manifest itself to us, it will be a delight to communicate even with that. And we may argue that if the beloved person is delayed a little on his way to Heaven by talking with us, he or she would be willing to make that sacrifice for our sake. The point overlooked here is, that on the astral, just as on the physical plane, it is a very easy thing to set up a bad habit. The soul in Kâma loca once slaking a thirst for earthly intercourse at the wells of mediumship will have a strong impulse to fall back again and again on that indulgence. We may be doing a great deal more than diverting the soul's attention from its own proper business by holding spiritualistic relations with it. We may be doing it serious and almost permanent injury. I am not affirming that this would invariably or generally be the case, but a severe view of the ethics of the subject must recognize the dangerous possibilities involved in the course of action under review. On the other hand, however, it is plain that cases may arise in which the desire for communication chiefly asserts itself from the other side: that is to say, in which the departed soul is laden with some unsatisfied desire - pointing possibly towards the fulfilment of some neglected duty on earth - the attention to which on the part of still-living friends may have an effect quite the reverse of that attending the mere encouragement of the Kâma loca entity in the resumption of its old earthly interests. In such cases the living friends may, by falling in with its desire to communicate, be the means, indirectly, of smoothing the path of its spiritual progress. Here again, however, we must be on our guard against the delusive aspect of appearances. A wish manifested by an inhabitant of Kâma loca may not always be the expression of an idea then operative in his mind. It may be the echo of an old, perhaps of a very old, desire, then for the first time finding a channel for its outward expression. In this way, although it would be reasonable to treat as important an intelligible wish conveyed to us from Kâma loca by a person only lately deceased, it would be prudent to regard with great suspicion such a wish emanating from the shade of a person who had been dead a long time, and whose general demeanour as a shade did not seem to convey the notion that he retained any vivid consciousness of his old personality.

The recognition of all these facts and possibilities of Kâma loca will, I think, afford theosophists a satisfactory explanation of a good many experiences connected with spiritualism which the first exposition of the esoteric doctrine, as bearing on this matter, left in much obscurity.

It will be readily perceived that as the soul slowly clears itself in Kâma loca of the affinities which retard its Devachanic development, the aspect it turns towards the earth is more and more enfeebled, and it is inevitable that there must always be in Kâma loca an enormous number of entities nearly ripe for a complete mergence in Devachan, who on that very account appear to an earthly observer in a state of advanced decrepitude. These will have sunk, as regards the activity of their lower astral principles, into the condition of the altogether vague and unintelligible entities, which, following the example of older occult writers, I have referred to as "shells" in the text of this chapter. The designation, however, is not altogether a happy one. It might have been better to have followed another precedent, and to have called them "shades," but either way their condition would be the same. All the vivid consciousness inhering, as they left the earth, in the principles appropriately related to the activities of physical life, has been transferred to the higher principles which do not manifest at seances. Their memory of earth-life has almost become extinct. Their lower principles are in such cases only reawakened by the influences of the mediumistic current into which they may be drawn, and they become then little more than astral lookingglasses, in which the thoughts of the medium or sitters at the seance are reflected. If we can imagine the colours on a painted canvas sinking by degrees into the substance of the material, and at last reemerging in their pristine brilliancy on the other side, we shall be conceiving a process which might not have destroyed the picture, but which would leave a gallery in which it took place, a dreary scene of brown and meaningless backs, and that is very much what the Kâma loca entities become before they ultimately shed the very material on which their first astral consciousness operated, and pass into the wholly purified Devachanic condition.

But this is not the whole of the story which teaches us to regard manifestations coming from Kâma loca with distrust. Our present comprehension of the subject enables us to realize that when the time arrives for that second death on the astral plane, which releases the purified Ego from Kâma loca altogether and sends it onward to the Devachanic state - something is left behind in Kâma loca which corresponds to the dead body bequeathed to the earth when the soul takes its first flight from physical existence. A dead astral body is in fact left behind in Kâma loca, and there is certainly no impropriety in applying the epithet "shell" to that residuum. The true shell in that state disintegrates in Kâma loca before very long, just as the true body left to the legitimate processes of Nature on earth would soon decay and blend its elements with the general reservoirs of matter of the order to which they belong. But until that disintegration is accomplished, the shell which the real Ego has altogether abandoned, may even in that state be mistaken sometimes at spiritual seances for a living entity. It remains for a time an astral looking-glass, in which mediums may see their own thoughts reflected, and take these back, fully believing them to come from an external source.

These phenomena in the truest sense of the term are galvanized astral corpses; none the less so, because until they are actually disintegrated a certain subtle connection will subsist between them and the true Devachanic spirit; just as such a subtle communication subsists in the first instance between the Kâma loca entity, and the dead body left on earth. That last-mentioned communication is kept up by the finely-diffused material of the original third principle, or *linga sharira*, and a study of this branch of the subject will, I believe, lead us up to a better comprehension than we possess at present of the circumstances under which materializations are sometimes accomplished at spiritual seances. But without going into that digression now, it is enough to recognize that the analogy may help to show how, between the Devachanic entity and the discarded shell in Kâma loca a similar connection may continue for awhile, acting, while it lasts, as a drag on the higher spirit, but perhaps as an after-glow of sunset on the shell. It would surely be distressing, however, in the highest degree, to any living friend of the person concerned, to get, through clairvoyance, or in any other way, sight or cognition of such a shell, and to be led into mistaking it for the true entity.

The comparatively clear view of Kâma loca which we are now enabled to take, may help us to employ terms relating to its phenomena with more precision than we have hitherto been able to attain. I think if we adopt one new expression, "astral soul," as applying to the entities in Kâma loca who have recently quitted earth-life, or who for other reasons still retain, in the aspect they turn back towards earth, a large share of the intellectual attributes that distinguished them on earth, we shall then find the other terms in use already, adequate to meet our remaining emergencies. Indeed, we may then get rid entirely of the inconvenient term "elementary," liable to be confused with elemental, and singularly inappropriate to the beings it describes. I would suggest that the astral soul as it sinks (regarded from our point of view) into intellectual decrepitude, should be spoken of in its faded condition as a shade, and that the term shell should be reserved for the true shells or astral dead bodies which the Devachanic *spirit* has finally quitted.

We are naturally led in studying the law of spiritual growth in Kâma loca to inquire how long a time may probably elapse before the transfer of consciousness from the lower to the higher principles of the astral soul may be regarded as complete; and as usual, when we come to figures relating to the higher processes of Nature, the answer is very elastic. But I believe the esoteric teachers of the East declare that as regards the average run of humanity - for what may be called, in a spiritual sense, the great middle classes of humanity - it is unusual that a Kâma loca entity will be in a position to manifest as such for more than twenty-five to thirty years. But on each side of this average the figures may run up very considerably. That is to say, a very ignoble and besotted human creature may hang about in Kâma loca for a much longer time for want of any higher principles sufficiently developed to take up his consciousness at all, and at the other end of the scale the very intellectual and mentally-active soul may remain for very long periods in Kâma loca (in the absence of spiritual affinities in corresponding force), by reason of the great persistence of forces and causes generated on the higher plane of effects, though mental activity could hardly be divorced in this way from spirituality except in cases where it was exclusively associated with worldly ambition. Again, while Kâma loca periods may thus be prolonged beyond the average from various causes, they may sink to almost infinitesimal brevity when the spirituality of a person dying at a ripe old age, and at the close of a life which has legitimately fulfilled its purpose, is already far advanced.

There is one other important possibility connected with manifestations reaching us by the usual channels of communication with Kâma loca, which it is desirable to notice here, although from its nature the realization of such a possibility cannot be frequent. No recent students of theosophy can expect to know as yet very much about the conditions of existence which await adepts who relinquish the use of physical bodies on earth. The higher possibilities open to them appear to me quite beyond the reach of intellectual appreciation. No man is clever enough, by virtue of the mere cleverness seated in a living brain, to understand Nirvana; but it would appear that adepts in some cases elect to pursue a course lying midway between re-incarnation and the passage into Nirvana, and in the higher regions of Devachan; that is to say, in the *arupa* state of Devachan may await the slow advance of human evolution towards the exalted condition they have thus attained. Now an adept who has thus become a Devachanic spirit of the most elevated type would not be cut off by the conditions of his Devachanic state - as would be the case with a natural Devachanic spirit passing through that state on his way to reincarnation - from manifesting his influence on earth. His would certainly *not* be an influence which would make itself felt by the instrumentality of any physical signs to mixed audiences, but it is not impossible that a medium of the highest type - who would more properly be called a seer - might be thus influenced. By such an Adept spirit, some great men in the world's history may from time to time have been overshadowed and inspired, consciously or unconsciously as the case may have been.

The disintegration of shells in Kama-loca will inevitably suggest to any one who endeavours to comprehend the process at all, that there must be in Nature some general reservoirs of the matter appropriate to that sphere of existence, corresponding to the physical earth and its surrounding elements into which our own bodies are resigned at death. The grand mysteries on which this consideration impinges will claim a far more exhaustive investigation than we have yet been enabled to undertake; but one broad idea connected with them may usefully be put forward without further delay. The state of Kama-loca is one which has its corresponding orders of matter in manifestation round it. I will not here attempt to go into the metaphysics of the problem, which might even lead us to discard the notion that astral matter need be any less real and tangible than that which appeals to our physical senses. It is enough for the present to explain that the propinquity of Kâma Loca to the earth which is so readily made apparent by spiritualistic experience, is explained by Oriental teaching to arise from this fact, - that Kama-loca is just as much in and of the earth as, during our lives, our astral soul is in and of the living man. The stage of Kama-loca, in fact, the great realm of matter in the appropriate state which constitutes Kamaloca and is perceptible to the senses of astral entities, as also to those of many clairvoyants, is the fourth principle of man. For the earth has its seven principles like the human creatures who inhabit it. Thus, the Devachanic state corresponds to the fifth principle of the earth, and Nirvana to the sixth principle.

# CHAPTER VII

## The Human Tide-Wave

A general account has already been given of the way in which the great evolutionary life-wave sweeps round and round the seven worlds which compose the planetary chain of which our earth is a part. Further assistance may now be offered, with the view of expanding this general idea into a fuller comprehension of the processes to which it relates. And no one additional chapter of the great story will do more towards rendering its character intelligible, than an explanation of certain phenomena connected with the progress of worlds, that may be conveniently called obscurations.

Students of occult philosophy who enter on that pursuit with minds already abundantly furnished in other ways, are very liable to misinterpret its earlier statements. Everything cannot be said at once, and the first broad explanations are apt to suggest conceptions in regard to details which are most likely to be erroneous with the most active-minded and intelligent thinkers. Such readers are not content with shadowy outlines even for a moment. Imagination fills in the picture, and if its work is undisturbed for any length of time, its author will be surprised afterwards to find that later information is incompatible with that which he had come to regard as having been distinctly taught in the beginning. Now in this treatise the writer's effort is to convey the information in such a way that hasty weed growths of the mind may be prevented as far as possible, but in this very effort it is necessary sometimes to run on quickly in advance, leaving some details, even very important details, to be picked up during a second journey over the old ground. So now the reader must be good enough to go back to the explanation given in Chapter III of the evolutionary progress through the whole planetary chain.

Some few words were said then concerning manner in which the life impulse passed on from planet to planet in "rushes or gushes; not by an even continuous flow." Now the course of evolution in its earlier stages is so far continuous that the preparation of several planets for the final tidal-wave of humanity may be going on simultaneously. Indeed, the preparation of all the seven planets may, at one stage of the proceedings, be going on simultaneously but the important point to remember is, that the main wave of evolution - the foremost growing wave - cannot be in more than one place at any time. The process goes on in the way which may now be described, and which the reader may be the better able to follow, if he constructs either on paper or in his own mind a diagram consisting of seven circles (representing the worlds) arranged on a ring. Calling them A,B,C &c., it will be observed from what has been already stated that circle (or globe)

D stands for our earth. Now the kingdoms of Nature as known to occultists, be it remembered, are seven in number, three having to do with astral and elementary forces, preceding the grosser material kingdoms in the order of their development. Kingdom 1 evolves on globe A, and passes on to B, as kingdom 2 begins to involve on A. Carry out this system and of course it will be seen that kingdom 1 is evolving on globe G, while kingdom 7, the human kingdom, is evolving on globe A. But now what happens as kingdom 7 passes on to globe B. There is no eighth kingdom to engage the activities of globe A. The great processes of evolution have culminated in the final tidal-wave of humanity, which, as it sweeps on, leaves a temporary lethargy of Nature behind. When the life-wave goes on to B, in fact, globe A passes for the time into a state of obscuration. This state is not one of decay, dissolution, or anything that can be properly called death. Decay itself, though its aspect is apt to mislead the mind, is a condition of activity in a certain direction, this consideration affording a clue to the meaning of a great deal which is otherwise meaningless, in that part of Hindu mythology which relates to the deities presiding over destruction. The obscuration of a world is a total suspension of its activity; this does not mean that the moment the last human monad passes on from any given world, that world is paralyzed by any convulsion, or subsides into the enchanted trance of a sleeping palace. The animal and vegetable life goes on as before, for a time, but its character begins to recede instead of advancing. The great lifewave has left it, and the animal and vegetable kingdoms gradually return to the condition in which they were found when the great life-wave first reached them. Enormous periods of time are available for this slow process by which the obscured world settled into sleep, for it will be seen that obscuration in each case lasts six times [Or we may say five times, allowing for the half period of morning which precedes and the half period of evening which follows the day of full activity.] as long as the period of each world's occupation by the human life-wave. That is to say, the process which is accomplished as above described in connection with the passage of the life-wave from globe A to globe B, is repeated all along the chain. When the wave passes to C, B is left in obscuration as well as A. Then D receives the lifewave, and A. B. C, are in obscuration. When the wave reaches G, all the preceding six worlds are in obscuration. Meanwhile the life-wave passes on in a certain regular progression, the symmetrical character of which is very satisfactory to scientific instincts. The reader will be prepared to pick up the idea at once, in view of the explanations already given of the way in which humanity evolves through seven great races during each round period on a planet - that is to say, during the occupation of such planet by the tidal wave of life. The fourth race is obviously the middle race of the series. As soon as this middle point is turned, and the evolution of the fifth race on any given planet begins, the preparation for humanity begins on the next. The evolution of the fifth race on E for example, is commensurate with the evolution, or rather with the revival, of the mineral kingdom on D, and so on. That is to say, the evolution of the sixth race on D, coincides with the revival of the vegetable kingdom on E, the seventh race on D, with the revival of the animal kingdom on E, and then when the last monads of the seventh race on D have passed into the subjective state or world of effects, the human period on E begins, and the first race begins its development there. Meanwhile the twilight period on the world preceding D has been deepening into the night of obscuration in the same progressive way, and obscuration there definitely sets in when the human period on D passes its half-way point. But just as the heart of a man beats and respiration continues, no matter how profound his sleep, there are processes of vital action which go on in the resting world even during the most profound depths of its repose. And these preserve, in view of the next return of the human wave, the results of the evolution that preceded its first arrival. Recovery for the re-awaking planet is a larger process than its subsidence into rest, for it has to attain a higher degree of perfection against the return of the human life-wave, than that at which it was left when the wave last went onward from its shore. But with every new beginning, Nature is infused with a vigour of its own - the freshness of a morning - and the later obscuration period, which is a time of preparation and hopefulness as it were, invests evolution itself with a new momentum. By the time the great life-wave returns, all is ready for its reception.

In the first essay on this subject it was roughly indicated that the various worlds making up our planetary chain were not all of the same materiality. Putting the conception of spirit at the north pole of the circle and that of matter at the south pole, the worlds of the descending arc vary in materiality and spirituality, like those of the ascending arc. This variation must now be considered more attentively if the reader wishes to realize the whole processes of evolution more fully than heretofore.

Besides the earth, which is at the lowest material point, there are only two other worlds of our chain which are visible to physical eyes - the one behind and the one in advance of it. These two worlds, as a matter of fact, are Mars and Mercury - Mars being behind and Mercury in advance of us - Mars in a state of entire obscuration now as regards the human life-wave, Mercury just beginning to prepare for its next human period. [It may be worth while here to remark for the benefit of people who may be disposed, from physical science reading, to object that Mercury is too near the Sun, and consequently too hot to be a suitable place of habitation for Man, - that in the official report of the Astronomical Department of the United States on the recent "Mount Whitney observations," statements will be found that may check too confident criticisms of occult science along that line. The results of the Mount Whitney observations on selective absorption of solar rays showed, according to the official reporter, that it would no longer be impossible to suggest the conditions of an atmosphere which would render Mercury habitable, at the one extreme of the scale, and Saturn at the other. We have no concern with Saturn at present, nor if it were necessary to explain on occult principles the habitability of Mercury, should the task be attempted with calculations about selective absorption. The fact is that ordinary science makes at once too much and two little of the Sun, as the storehouse of force for the solar system, - too much in so far as the heat of planets has a great deal to do with another influence quite distinct from the Sun, and influence which will not be thoroughly understood till more is known than at present about the correlations of heat and magnetism, and of the magnetic, meteoric dust, with which interplanetary space is pervaded. However it is enough - to rebut any objection that might be raised against the explanation now in progress, from the point of view of loyal devotees of last year's science - to point out that such objections would be already out of date. Modern science is very progressive, - this is one of its greatest merits, - but it is not a meritorious habit with modern scientists to think, at each stage of its progress, that all conceptions incompatible with that stage must necessarily be absurd.]

The two planets of our chain that are behind Mars, and the two that are in advance of Mercury, are not composed of an order of matter which telescopes can take cognizance of. Four out of the seven are thus of an ethereal nature, which people who can only conceive matter in its earthly form will be inclined to call immaterial. But they are not really immaterial at all. They are simply in a finer state of materiality than the earth, but their finer state does not in any way defeat the uniformity of Nature's design in regard to the methods and stages of their evolution. Within the scale of their subtle "invisibility," the successive rounds and races of mankind pass through their stages of greater and less materiality just as on this earth; but whoever would comprehend them must comprehend this earth first, and work out their delicate phenomena by correspondential inferences. Let us return therefore to the consideration of the great lifewave in its aspects on this planet.

Just as the chain of worlds treated as a unity has its north and south, its spiritual and material pole, working from spirituality down through materiality up to spirituality again, so the rounds of mankind constitute a similar series which the chain of globes itself might be taken to symbolize. In the evolution of man in fact, on any one plane as on all, there is a descending and an ascending arc; spirit, so to speak, involving itself into matter, and matter evolving itself into spirit. The lowest or most material point, in the cycle thus becomes the inverted apex of physical intelligence, which is the masked manifestation of spiritual intelligence. Each round of mankind evolved on the downward arc (as each race of each round if we descend to the smaller mirror of the cosmos) must thus be more physically intelligent than its predecessor, and each in the upward arc must be invested with a more refined form of mentality commingled with greater spiritual intuitiveness. In the first round therefore we find man, a relatively ethereal being compared even on earth with the state he has now attained here, not intellectual, but super-spiritual. Like the animal and vegetable shapes around him, he inhabits an immense but loosely organized body. In the second round he is still gigantic and ethereal, but growing firmer and more condensed in body - a more physical man, but still, less intelligent than spiritual. In the third round he has developed a perfectly concrete and compacted body, at first the form rather of a giant ape than of a true man, but with intelligence coming more and more into the ascendant. In the last half of the third round his gigantic stature decreases, his body improves in texture, and he begins to be a rational man. In the fourth round intellect, now fully developed, achieves enormous progress. The earliest races with which the round begins, acquire human speech as we understand it. The world teems with the results of intellectual activity and spiritual decline. At the halfway point of the fourth round here, the polar point of the whole seven-world period is passed. From this point outwards the spiritual Ego begins its real struggle with body and mind to manifest its transcendental powers. In the fifth round the struggle continues, but the transcendental faculties are largely developed, though the struggle between these on the one hand with physical intellect and propensity is fiercer than ever, for the intellect of the fifth round, as well as its spirituality, is an advance on that of the fourth. In the sixth round humanity attains a degree of perfection both of body and soul, of intellect and spirituality, which ordinary mortals of the present epoch will not readily realize in their imaginations. The most supreme combinations of wisdom, goodness, and transcendental enlightenment which the world has ever seen or thought of, will represent the ordinary type of manhood. Those faculties which now, in the rare efflorescence of a generation, enable some extraordinary gifted persons to explore the mysteries of Nature and gather the knowledge of which some crumbs are now being offered (through these writings and in other ways) to the ordinary world, will then be the common appanage of all. As to what the seventh round will be like, the most communicative occult teachers are solemnly silent. Mankind in the seventh round will be something altogether too God-like for mankind in the fourth round to forecast its attributes.

During the occupation of any planet by the human life-wave, each individual monad is inevitably incarnated many times. This has been partly explained. If one existence only be passed by the monad in each of the branch races through which it must pass at least once, the total number accomplished during a round period on one planet, would be 343 - the third power of seven. But as a matter of fact each monad is incarnated twice in each of the branch races, and also comes in, necessarily, for some few extra incarnations as well. For reasons which are not easy for the outsider to divine, the possessors of occult knowledge are especially reluctant to give out numerical facts relating to cosmogony, though it is hard for the uninitiated to understand why these should be withheld. At present, for example, we shall not be able to state what is the actual duration in years of the round period. But a concession, which only those who have long been students of occultism by the old method will fully appreciate, has been made about the numbers with which we are immediately concerned; and this concession is valuable at all events, as it helps to elucidate an interesting fact connected with evolution, on the threshold of which we have now arrived. This fact is, that while the earth, for example, is inhabited as at present, by fourth round humanity, by the wave of human life, that is to say, on its fourth journey round the circle of the worlds, there may be present among us some few persons, few in relation to the total number, who, properly speaking, belong to the fifth round. Now, in the sense of the term at present employed, it must not be supposed that by any miraculous process, any individual unit has actually traveled round the whole chain of worlds once more often than his compeers. Under the explanations just given as to the way the tide-wave of humanity progresses, it will be seen that this is impossible. Humanity has not yet paid its fourth visit even, to the planet next in advance of our own. But individual monads may outstrip their companions as regards their individual development, and so become exactly as mankind generally will be when the fifth round has been fully evolved. And this may be accomplished in two ways. A man born as an ordinary fourth round man, may, by processes of occult training, convert himself into a man having all the attributes of a fifth round man, and so become what we may call an artificial fifth rounder. But independently of all exertions made by man in his present incarnation, a man may also be born a fifth rounder, though in the midst of fourth round humanity, by virtue of the total number of his previous incarnations.

It x stands for the normal number of incarnations which in the course of Nature a monad must go through during a round period on one planet, and y for the margin of extra incarnations into which by a strong desire for physical life he may force himself during such a period, then, as a matter of fact, $24 1/2 (x + y)$ may exceed $28x$; that is to say, in $3 1/2$ rounds a monad may have accomplished as many incarnations as an ordinary monad would have accomplished in four complete rounds. In less than $3 1/2$ rounds the result could not have been attained, so that it is only now that we have passed the halfway point of evolution on this halfway planet, that the fifth rounders are beginning to drop in.

It is not possible in the nature of things that a monad can do more than outstrip his companions by more than one round. This consideration notwithstanding, Buddha was a sixth round man, but this fact has to do with a great mystery outside the limits of the present calculation. Enough for the moment to say that the evolution of a Buddha has to do with something more than mere incarnations within the limits of one planetary chain.

Since large numbers of lives have been recognized in the above calculations as following one another in the successive incarnations of an individual monad, it is important here, with the view of averting misconceptions, to point out that the periods of time over which these incarnations range are so great, that vast intervals separate them, numerous as they are. As stated above, we cannot just now give the actual duration of the round periods. Nor, indeed could any figures be quoted as indicating the duration of all round periods equally, for these vary in length within very wide limits. But here is a simple fact which has been definitely stated on the highest occult authority we are concerned with. The present race of humanity, the present fifth race of the fourth round period, began to evolve about one million of years ago. Now it is not yet finished; but supposing that a million years had constituted the complete life of the race, [The complete life of a race is certainly much longer than this; but when we get to figures of this kind we are on very delicate ground, for precise periods are very profound secrets, for reasons uninitiated students ("lay chelas," as the adepts now say, coining a new designation to meet a new condition of things) can only imperfectly divine. Calculations like those given above may be trusted literally as far as they go, but must not rashly be made the basis of others.] how would it have been divided up for each individual monad? In a race there must be rather more than 100, and there can hardly be 120 incarnations for an individual monad. But say even there have been already 120 incarnations for monads in the present race already. And say that the average life of each incarnation was a century, even then we should only have 12,000 years out of the million spent in physical existence against 988.000 years spent in the subjective sphere, or there would be an average of more than 8000 years between each incarnation. Certainly these intervening periods are of very variable length, but they can hardly ever contract to anything less than 1500 years - leaving out of account of course the case of adepts who have placed themselves quite outside the operation of the ordinary law - and 1500 years if not an impossibly short, would be a very brief interval between two rebirths.

These calculations must be qualified by one of two considerations, however. The cases of children dying in infancy are quite unlike those of persons who attain full maturity, and for obvious reasons, that the explanations now already given will suggest, A child, dying before it has lived long enough to begin to be responsible for its actions, has generated no fresh Karma. The spiritual monad leaves that child's body in just the same state in which it entered it after its last death in Devachan. It has had no opportunity of playing on its new instrument, which has been broken before even it was tuned. A re-incarnation of the monad, therefore, may take place immediately on the line of its old attraction. But the monad so reincarnated is not to be spiritually identified in any way with the dead child. So, in the same way, with a monad getting into the body of a born idiot. The instrument cannot be tuned, so it cannot play on that any more than on the child's body in the first few years of childhood. But both these cases are manifest exceptions that do not alter the broad rule above laid down for all persons attaining maturity, and living their earth lives for good or evil.

## Annotations

Later information and study - the comparison, that is to say, of the various branches of the doctrine, and the collocation of other statements with those in the foregoing chapter - show the difficulty of applying figures to the Esoteric Doctrines in a very striking light. Figures may be quite trustworthy as representing broad averages, and yet very misleading when applied to special cases. Devachanic periods vary for different people within such very wide limits that any rule laid down in the matter must be subject to a bewildering cloud of exceptions. To begin with, the average mentioned above has no doubt been computed with reference to fully matured adults. Between the quite young child who has no Devachanic period at all and the adult who accomplishes an average period we have to take note of persons dying in youth, who have accumulated *Karma*, and who must therefore pass through the usual stages of spiritual development, but for whom the brief lives they have spent have not produced causes which take very long to work themselves out. Such persons would return to incarnation after a sojourn in the world of effects of corresponding brevity. Again there are such things as artificial incarnations accomplished by the direct intervention of the Mahatmas when a *chela* who may not yet have acquired anything resembling the power of controlling the matter himself, is brought back into incarnation almost immediately after his previous physical death, without having been suffered to float into the current of natural causes at all. Of course in such cases it may be said that the claims the person concerned has established on the Mahatmas are themselves natural causes of a kind, the intervention of the Mahatmas, who are quite beyond the liability of acting capriciously in such a matter, being so much fruit of effort in the preceding life, so much Karma. But still either way such cases would be equally withdrawn from the operation of the general average rule.

Clearly it is impossible when the complicated facts of an entirely unfamiliar science are being presented to untrained minds for the first time, to put them forward with all their appropriate qualifications, compensations and abnormal developments visible from the beginning. We must be content to take the broad rules first and deal with the exceptions afterwards, and especially is this the case with occult study, in connection with which the traditional methods of teaching, generally followed, aim at impressing every fresh idea on the memory, by provoking the perplexity it at last relieves. In relation to another matter dealt with in the preceding pages, an important exception in Nature has thus, it seems to me now, been left out of account. The description I have given of the progress of the human tide-wave is quite coherent as it stands, but since the publication of the original edition of this book some criticism was directed, in India, to a comparison between my version of the story and certain passages in other writings, known to emanate from a Mahatma. A discrepancy between the two statements was pointed out, the other version assuming the possibility that a monad actually *might* have traveled round the seven planets once more often than the compeers among whom he might ultimately find himself on this earth. My account of the obscurations appears to render this contingency impossible. The clue to the mystery appears to lie outside the domain of those facts concerning which the adepts are willing to speak freely; and the reader must clearly understand that the explanation I am about to offer is the fruit of my own speculation and comparison of different parts of the doctrine - not authentic information received from the author of my general teaching.

The fact appears to be that the obscurations are so far complete as to present all the phenomena above described in regard to each planet they affect *as a whole*. But exceptional phenomena for which we must be ever on the alert, come into play even in this matter. The great bulk of humanity is driven on from one planet to the next by the great cyclic impulse when its time comes for such a transition, but the planet it quits is not *utterly* denuded of humanity, nor is it, in *every* region of its surface rendered, by the physical and climatic changes that come on, unfit to be the habitation of human beings. Even during obscuration a small colony of humanity clings to each planet, and the monads associated with these small colonies following different laws of evolution, and beyond the reach of those attractions which govern the main vortex of humanity in the planet occupied by the great tide-wave, pass on from world to world along what may be called the inner round of evolution, far ahead of the race at large. What may be the circumstances which occasionally project a soul even from the midst of the great human vortex, right out of the attraction of the planet occupied by the tide wave, and into the attraction of the Inner Round - is a question that can only be a subject for us at present of very uncertain conjecture.

It may be worth while to draw attention, in connection with the solution I have ventured to offer as applicable to the problem of the Inner Rounds to the way in which the fact of Nature I assume to exist, would harmonize with the widely diffused doctrines of the Deluge. That portion of a planet which remained habitable during an obscuration would be equivalent to the Noah's Ark of the biblical narrative taken in its largest symbolical meaning. Of course the narrative of the Deluge has minor symbolical meanings also, but it does not appear improbable that the Kabalists should also have associated with it, the larger significance now suggested. In due time when the obscured planet grew ready once more to receive a full population of humanity, the colonists of the ark would be ready to commence the process of populating it afresh.

# CHAPTER VIII

## The Progress of Humanity

The course of Nature provides, as the reader will now have seen, for the indefinite progress towards higher phases of existence of all human entities. But no less will it have been seen that by endowing these entities, as they advance with ever-increasing faculties and by constantly enlarging the scope of their activity. Nature also furnishes each human entity with more and more decisive opportunities of choosing between good and evil. In the earlier rounds of humanity this privilege of selection is not fully developed, and responsibility of action is correspondingly incomplete. The earlier rounds of humanity, in fact, do not invest the Ego with spiritual responsibility at all in the larger sense of the term which we are now approaching. The Devachanic periods which follow each objective existence in turn, dispose fully of its merits and demerits, and the most deplorable personality which the ego during the first half of its evolution can possible develop, is merely dropped out of the account as regards the larger undertaking, while the erring personality itself pays its relatively brief penalty, and troubles Nature no more. But the second half of the great evolutionary period is carried on on different principles. The phases of existence which are now coming into view, cannot be entered upon by the ego without positive merits of its own appropriate to the new developments in prospect; it is not enough that the now fully responsible and highly gifted being which man becomes at the great turning-point in his career, should float idly on the stream of progress; he must begin to swim, if he wishes to push his way forward.

Debarred by the complexity of the subject from dealing with all its features simultaneously, our survey of Nature has so far contemplated the seven rounds of human development, which constitute the whole planetary undertaking with which we are concerned, as a continuous series, throughout which it is the natural destiny of humanity in general to pass. But it will be remembered that humanity in the sixth round has been spoken of as so highly developed that the sublime attributes and faculties of the highest adeptship are the common appanage of all; while in the seventh round the race has almost emerged from humanity into divinity. Now every human being in this state of development will still be identified by an uninterrupted connection with all the personalities which have been strung upon that thread of life from the beginning of the great evolutionary process. Is it conceivable that the character of such personalities is of no consequence in the long-run, and that two God-like beings might stand side by side in the seventh round, developed, the one from a long series of blameless and serviceable existences, the other from an equally long series of evil and grovelling lives? That surely could not come to pass, and we have to ask now, how do we find the congruities of Nature preserved compatibly with the appointed evolution of humanity to the higher forms of existence which crown the edifice?

Just as childhood is irresponsible for its acts, the earlier races of humanity are irresponsible for theirs; but there comes the period of full growth, when the complete development of the faculties which enable the individual man to choose between good and evil, in the single life with which he is for the moment concerned, enable the continuous ego also to make its final selection. That period - that enormous period, for Nature is in no hurry to catch its creatures in a trap in such a matter as this - is barely yet beginning, and a complete round period around the seven worlds will have to be gone through before it is over. Until the middle of the fifth period is passed on this earth, the great question - to be or not to be for the future - is not irrevocably settled. We are coming now into the possession of the faculties which render man a fully responsible being, but we have yet to employ those faculties during the maturity of our ego-hood in the manner which shall determine the vast consequences hereafter.

It is during the first half of the fifth round that the struggle principally takes place. Till then, the ordinary course of life may be a good or a bad preparation for the struggle, but cannot fairly be described as the struggle itself. And now we have to examine the nature of the struggle, so far merely spoken of as the selection between good and evil. That is in no way an inaccurate, but it is an incomplete, definition.

The ever-recurring and ever-threatened conflict between intellect and spirituality, is the phenomenon to be now examined. The commonplace conceptions which these two words denote, must of course be expanded to some extent before the occult conception is realized; for European habits of thinking are rather apt to set up in the mind an ignoble image of spirituality, as an attribute rather of the character than of the mind itself, - a pale goody-goodiness, born of an attachment to religious ceremonial and of devout aspirations, no matter to what whimsical notions of Heaven and Divinity in which the "spiritually-minded" person may have been brought up. Spirituality, in the occult sense, has little or nothing to do with feeling devout; it has to do with the capacity of the mind for assimilating knowledge at the fountain-head of knowledge itself - of absolute knowledge - instead of by the circuitous and labourious process of ratiocination.

The development of pure intellect, the ratiocinative faculty, has been the business of European nations for so long, and in this department of human progress they have achieved such magnificent triumphs, that nothing in occult philosophy will be less acceptable to Europeans themselves at first, and while the ideas at stake are imperfectly grasped, than the first aspect of the occult theory concerning intellect and spirituality; but this does not arise so much from the undue tendency of occult science to depreciate intellect, as from the undue tendency of modern Western speculation to depreciate spirituality. Broadly speaking, so far Western philosophy has had no opportunity of appreciating spirituality; it has not been made acquainted with the range of the inner faculties of man; it has merely groped blindly in the direction of a belief that such inner faculties existed; and Kant himself, the greatest modern exponent of that idea, does little more than contend that there is such a faculty as intuition - if we only knew how to work with it.

The process of working with it, is occult science in its highest aspect, the cultivation of spirituality. The cultivation of mere power over the forces of Nature, the investigation of some of her subtler secrets as regards the inner principles controlling physical results, is occult science in its lowest aspect, and into that lower region of its activity mere physical science may, or even must, gradually run up. But the acquisition by mere intellect - physical science *in excelsis* - of privileges which are the proper appanage of spirituality, - is one of the dangers of that struggle which decides the ultimate destiny of the human ego. For there is one thing which intellectual processes do not help mankind to realize, and that is the nature and supreme excellence of spiritual existence. On the contrary, intellect arises out of physical causes - the perfection of the physical brain - and tends only to physical results, the perfection of material welfare. Although, as a concession to "weak brethren" and "religion" on which it looks with good-humoured contempt, modern intellect does not condemn spirituality, it certainly treats the physical human life as the only serious business with which grave men, or even earnest philanthropists, can concern themselves. But obviously, if spiritual existence, vivid subjective consciousness, really does go on for periods greater than the periods of intellectual physical existence in the ratio, as we have seen in discussing the Devachanic condition, of 80 to 1 at least, then surely man's subjective existence is more important than his physical existence, and intellect is in error when all its efforts are bent on the amelioration of the physical existence.

These considerations show how the choice between good and evil - which has been made by the human ego in the course of the great struggle between intellect and spirituality - is not a mere choice between ideas so plainly contrasted as wickedness and virtue. It is not so rough a question as that - whether man be wicked or virtuous - which must really at the final critical turning-point decide whether he shall continue to live and develop into higher phases of existence, or cease to live altogether. The truth of the matter is (if it is not imprudent at this stage of our progress to brush the surface of a new mystery) that the question, to be or not to be, is not settled by reference to the question whether a man be wicked or virtuous at all. It will plainly be seen eventually that there must be evil spirituality as well as good spirituality. So that the great question of continued existence turns altogether and of necessity on the question of spirituality, as compared with physicality. The point is not so much "*shall* a man live, is he good enough to be permitted to live any longer?" as "*can* the man live any longer in the higher levels of existence into which humanity must at last evolve? Has he qualified himself to live by the cultivation of the durable portion of his nature? If not, he has got to the end of his tether.

It need not be hurriedly supposed that occult philosophy considers vice and virtue of no consequence to human spiritual destinies, because it does not discover in Nature that these characteristics determine ultimate progress in evolution. No system is so pitilessly inflexible in its morality as the system which occult philosophy explores and expounds. But that which vice and virtue of themselves determine, is happiness and misery, not the final problem of continued existence, beyond that immeasurably distant period, when in the progress of evolution man has got to begin being something more than man, and cannot go on along the path of progress with the help only of the relatively lower human attributes. It is true again that one can hardly imagine virtue in any decided degree to fail in engendering, in due time, the required higher attributes, but we should not be scientifically accurate in speaking of it as the cause of progress, in ultimate stages of elevation, though it may provoke the development of that which is the cause of progress.

This consideration - that ultimate progress is determined by spirituality irrespective of its moral colouring, is the great meaning of the occult doctrine that "to be immortal in good one must identify oneself with God; to be immortal in evil with Satan. These are the two poles of the world of souls; between these two poles vegetate and die without remembrance the useless portion of mankind" [Eliphas Levi]. The enigma, like all occult formulas, has a lesser application (fitting the microcosm as well as the macrocosm, and in its lesser significance refers to Devachan or Avitchi, and the blank destiny of colourless personalities; but in its more important bearing it relates to the final sorting out of humanity at the middle of the great fifth round, the annihilation of the utterly unspiritual Egos and the passage onward of the others to be immortal in good, or immortal in evil. Precisely the same meaning attaches to the passage in Revelation (iii 15, 16): "I would thou wert cold or hot; so then because thou art lukewarm, and neither cold nor hot, I will spue thee out of my mouth."

Spirituality, then, is not devout aspiration; it is the highest kind of intellection, that which takes cognizance of the workings of Nature by direct assimilation of the mind and her higher principles. The objection which physical intelligence will bring against this view is that the mind can cognize nothing except by observation of phenomena and reasoning thereon. That is the mistake - it can; and the existence of occult science is the highest proof thereof. But there are hints pointing in the direction of such proof all around us if we have but the patience to examine their true bearings. It is idle to say, in face, merely for one thing, of the phenomena of clairvoyance - crude and imperfect as those have been which have pushed themselves on the attention of the world - that there are no other avenues to consciousness but those of the five senses. Certainly in the ordinary world the clairvoyant faculty is an exceedingly rare one, but it indicates the existence in man of a potential faculty, the nature of which, as inferred from its slightest manifestations, must obviously be capable in its highest development of leading to a direct assimilation of knowledge independently of observation.

One of the most embarrassing difficulties that beset the present attempt to translate the esoteric doctrine into plain language, is due really to the fact, that spiritual perceptiveness, apart from all ordinary processes by which knowledge is acquired, is a great and grand possibility of human nature. It is by that method in the regular course of occult training that adepts impart instruction to their pupils. They awaken the dormant sense in the pupil, and through this they imbue his mind with a knowledge that such and such a doctrine is the real truth. The whole scheme of evolution, which the foregoing chapters have portrayed, infiltrates into the regular chela's mind by reason of the fact that he is made to see the process taking place by clairvoyant vision. There are no words used in his instruction at all. And adepts themselves to whom the facts and processes of Nature are familiar as our five fingers to us, find it difficult to explain in a treatise which they cannot illustrate for us, by producing mental pictures in our dormant sixth sense, the complex anatomy of the planetary system.

Certainly it is not to be expected that mankind as yet should be generally conscious of possessing the sixth sense, for the day of its activity has not yet come. It has been already stated that each round in turn is devoted to the perfection in man of the corresponding principle in its numerical order, and to its preparation for assimilation with the next. The earlier rounds have been described as concerned with man in a shadowy, loosely organized, unintelligent form. The first principle of all, the body, was developed, but it was merely growing used to vitality, and was unlike anything we can now picture to ourselves. The fourth round, in which we are now engaged, is the round in which the fourth principle, Will, Desire, is fully developed, and in which it is engaged in assimilating itself with the fifth principle, reason, intelligence. In the fifth round, the completely developed reason, intellect, or soul, in which the Ego then resides, must assimilate itself to the sixth principle, spirituality, or give up the business of existence altogether.

All readers of Buddhist literature are familiar with the constant references made there to the Arhat's union of his soul with God. This, in other words, is the premature development of his sixth principle. He forces himself right up through all the obstacles which impede such an operation in the case of a fourth round man, into that stage of evolution which awaits the rest of humanity - or rather so much of humanity as may reach it in the ordinary course of Nature - in the latter part of the fifth round. And in doing this it will be observed he tides himself right over the great period of danger - the middle of the fifth round. That is the stupendous achievement of the adept as regards his own personal interests. He has reached the further shore of the sea in which so many of mankind will perish. He waits there in a contentment which people cannot even realize without some glimmerings of spirituality - of the sixth sense - themselves for the arrival there of his future companions. He dos not wait in his physical body, let me hasten to add to avoid misconstruction, but when at last *privileged to resign this*, in a spiritual condition, which it would be foolish to attempt to describe, while even the Devachanic states of ordinary humanity are themselves almost beyond the reach of imaginations untrained in spiritual science.

But, returning to the ordinary course of humanity and the growth into sixth round people, of men and women who do not become adepts at any premature stage of their career, it will be observed that this *is* the ordinary course of Nature in one sense of the expression, but so also is it the ordinary course of Nature for every grain of corn that is developed to fall into appropriate soil, and grow up into an ear of corn itself. All the same a great many grains do nothing of the sort, and a great many human Egos will never pass through the trials of the fifth round. The final effort of Nature in evolving man is to evolve from him a being unmeasurably higher, to be a conscious agent, and what is ordinarily meant by a creative principle in Nature herself ultimately. The first achievement is to evolve free-will, and the next to perpetuate that free-will by inducing it to unite itself with the final purpose of Nature, which is good. In the course of such an operation it is inevitable that a great deal of the free-will evolved should turn to evil, and after producing temporary suffering, be dispersed and annihilated. More than this, the final purpose can only be achieved by a profuse expenditure of material, and just as this goes on in the lower stages of evolution, where a thousand seeds are thrown off by a vegetable, for every one that ultimately fructifies into a new plant, so are the god-like germs of Will, sown one in each man's breast, in abundance like the seeds blown about in the wind. Is the justice of Nature to be impugned by reason of the fact that many of these germs will perish? Such an idea could only rise in a mind that will not realize the room there is in Nature for the growth of every germ which chooses to grow, and to the extent it chooses to grow, be that extent great or small. If it seems to any one horrible that an "immortal soul" should perish, under any circumstances, that impression can only be due to the pernicious habit of regarding everything as eternity, which is not this microscopic life. There is room in the subjective spheres, and time in the catenary manvantara, before we even approach the Dhyan Chohan of God-like period, for more than the ordinary brain has every yet conceived of immortality. Every good deed and elevated impulse that every man or woman ever did or felt, must reverberate through aeons of spiritual existence, whether the human entity concerned proves able or not to expand into the sublime and stupendous development of the seventh round. And it is out of the causes generated in one of our brief lives on earth, that exoteric speculation conceives itself capable of constructing eternal results! Out of such a seven or eight hundredth part of our objective life on earth during the present stay here of the evolutionary life-wave, we are to expect Nature to discern sufficient reason for deciding upon our whole subsequent career. In truth, Nature will make such a large return for a comparatively small expenditure of human will-power in the right direction, that, extravagant as the expectation just stated may appear, and extravagant as it is applied to ordinary lives, one brief existence may sometimes suffice to anticipate the growth of milliards of years. The adept may in the one earth-life [In practice, my impression is that this is rarely achieved in one earth-life; approached rather in two or three artificial incarnations.] achieve so much advancement that his subsequent growth is certain, and merely a matter of time; but then the seed germ which produces an adept in our life, must be very perfect to begin with, and the early conditions of its growth favourable, and withal the effort on the part of the man himself, life-long and far more concentrated, more intense, more arduous, than it is possible for the uninitiated outsider to realize. In ordinary cases, the life which is divided between material enjoyment and spiritual aspiration - however sincere and beautiful the latter -can only be productive of a correspondingly duplex result, of a spiritual reward in Devachan, of a new birth on earth. The manner in which the adept gets above the necessity of such a new birth, is perfectly scientific and simple be it observed, though it sounds like a theological mystery when expounded in exoteric writings by reference to Karma and Skandhas, Trishna, and Tanha, and so forth. The next earth-life is as much a consequence of affinities engendered by the fifth principle, the continuous human soul, as the Devachanic experiences which come first are the growth of the thoughts and aspirations of an elevated character, which the person concerned has created during life. That is to say, the affinities engendered in ordinary cases are partly material, partly spiritual. Therefore they start the soul on its entrance into the world of effects with a double set of attractions inhering in it, one set producing the subjective consequences of its Devachanic life, the other set asserting themselves at the close of that life, and carrying the soul back again into re-incarnation. But if the person during his objective life absolutely develops no affinities for material existence, starts his soul at death with all its attractions tending one way in the direction of spirituality, and none at all drawing it back to objective life, it does not come back; it mounts into a condition of spirituality corresponding to the intensity of the attractions or affinities in that direction, and the other thread of connection is cut off.

Now this explanation does not entirely cover the whole position, because the adept himself, no matter how high, does return to incarnation eventually, after the rest of mankind have passed across the great dividing period in the middle of the fifth round. Until the exaltation of Planetary Spirithood is reached, the highest human soul must have a certain affinity for earth still, though not the earth-life of physical enjoyments and passions that we are going through. But the important point to realize in regard to the spiritual consequences of earthly life is, that in so large a majority of cases, that the abnormal few need not be talked about, the sense of justice in regard to the destiny of good men is amply satisfied by the course of Nature step by step as time advances. The spirit-life is ever at hand to receive, refresh, and restore the soul after the struggles, achievements, or sufferings of incarnation. And more than this, reserving the question about eternity, Nature, in the intercyclic periods at the apex of each round, provides for all mankind, except those unfortunate failures who have persistently adhered to the path of evil, great intervals of spiritual blessedness, far longer and more exalted in their character than the Devachanic periods of each separate life. Nature, in fact, is inconceivably liberal and patient to each and all her candidates for the final examination during their long preparation for this. Nor is one failure to pass even this final examination absolutely fatal. The failures may try again, if they are not utterly disgraceful failures, but they must wait for the next opportunity.

A complete explanation of the circumstances under which such waiting is accomplished, would not come into the scheme of this treatise; but it must not be supposed that candidates for progress, self-convicted of unfitness to proceed at the critical period of the fifth round, fall necessarily into the sphere of annihilation. For that attraction to assert itself, the Ego must have developed a positive attraction for matter, a positive repulsion for spirituality, which is overwhelming in its force. In the absence of such affinities, and in the absence also of such affinities as would suffice to tide the Ego over the great gulf, the destiny which meets the mere failures of Nature is, *as regards the present planetary manwantara*, to die, as Eliphas Levy puts it, without remembrance. They have lived their life, and had their share of Heaven, but they are not capable of ascending the tremendous altitudes of spiritual progress then confronting them. But they are qualified for further incarnation and life on the planes of existence to which they are accustomed. They will wait, therefore, in the negative spiritual state they have attained, till those planes of existence are again in activity in the *next planetary manwantara*. The duration of such waiting is, of course, beyond the reach of imagination altogether, and the precise nature of the existence which is now contemplated is no less unrealizable; but the broad pathway through that strange region of dreamy semi-animation must be taken note if, in order that the symmetry and completeness of the whole evolutionary scheme may be perceived.

And with this last contingency provided for, the whole scheme does lie before the reader *in its main outlines* with tolerable completeness. We have seen the one life, the spirit, animating matter in its lowest forms first, and evoking growth by slow degrees into higher forms. Individualizing itself at last in man, it works up through inferior and irresponsible incarnations until it has penetrated the higher principles, and evolved a true human soul, which is thenceforth the master of its own fate, though guarded in the beginning by natural provisions which debar it from premature shipwreck, which stimulate and refresh it on its course. But the ultimate destiny offered to that soul is to develop not only into a being capable of taking care of itself, but into a being capable of taking care also of others, of presiding over and directing, within what may be called constitutional limits, the operations of Nature herself. Clearly before the soul can have earned the right to that promotion, it must have been tried by having conceded to it full control over it own affairs. That full control necessarily conveys the power to shipwreck itself. The safeguards put round the Ego in its youth - its inability to get into the higher or lower states than those of inter-mundane Devachan and Avitchi - fall from it in its maturity. It is potent, then, over its own destinies, not only in regard to the development of transitory joy and suffering, but in regard to the stupendous opportunities in both directions which existence opens out before it. It may seize on the higher opportunities in two ways; it may throw up the struggle in two ways; it may attain sublime spirituality for good, or sublime spirituality for evil; it may ally itself to physically for (not evil, but for) utter annihilation; or, on the other hand, for (not good, but for) the negative result of beginning the educational processes of incarnation all over again.

## Annotations

The condition into which the monads failing to pass the middle of the fifth round must fall as the tide of evolution sweeps on, leaving them stranded, so to speak, upon the shores of time, is not described very fully in this chapter. By a few words only is it indicated that the failures of each manwantara are not absolutely annihilated when they reach "the end of their tether," but are destined after some enormous period of waiting to pass once more into the current of evolution. Many inferences may be deduced from this condition of things. The period of waiting which the failures have thus to undergo, is to begin with, a duration so stupendous as to baffle the imagination. The latter half of the fifth round, the whole of the sixth and seventh have to be performed by the successful graduates in spirituality, and the later rounds are of immensely longer duration than those of the middle period. Then follows the vast interval of Nirvanic rest, which closes the manwantara, the immeasurable Night of Brahma, the Pralaya of the whole planetary chain. Only when the next manwantara begins do the failures begin to wake from their awful trance - awful to the imagination of beings in the full activity of life, though such a trance, being necessarily all but destitute of consciousness, is possibly no more tedious than a dreamless night in the memory of profound sleeper. The fate of the failures may be grievous first of all, rather on account of what they miss, than on account of what they incur. Secondly, however, it is grievous on account of that to which it leads, for all the trouble of physical life and almost endless incarnations must be gone through afresh, when the failures wake up; whereas the perfected beings, who outstripped them in evolution during that fifth round in which they become failures, will have grown into the god-like perfection of Dhyan Chohan-hood during their trance, and will be the presiding geniuses of the next manwantara, not its helpless subjects.

Apart altogether, meanwhile, from what may be regarded as the personal interest of the entities concerned, the existence of the failures in Nature at the beginning of each manwantara is a fact which contributes in a very important degree to a comprehension of the evolutionary system. When the planetary chain is first of all evolved out of chaos - if we may use such an expression as "first of all" in a qualified sense, having regard to the reflection that "in the beginning" is a mere *facon de parler* applied to any period in eternity - there are no failures to deal with. Then the descent of spirit into matter, through the elemental, mineral, and other kingdoms, goes on in the way already described in earlier chapters of this book. But from the second manwantara of a planetary chain, during the activity of the solar system, which provides for many such manwantaras, the course of events is somewhat different - easier, if I may again be allowed to use an expression that is applicable rather in a conversational than severely scientific sense. At any rate it is quicker, for human entities are already in existence, ready to enter into incarnation as soon as the world, also already in existence, can be got ready for them. The truth thus appears to be, that after the first manwantara of a series - enormously longer in duration than its successors - no entities, then first evolved from quite the lower kingdoms, do more than attain the threshold of humanity. The late failures pass into incarnation, and then eventually the surviving animal entities already differentiated. But, compared with the passages in the esoteric doctrine which affect the current evolution of our own race, these considerations, relating to the very early periods of world- evolution, have little more than an intellectual interest, and cannot as yet by any contributions of mine be very greatly amplified.

# CHAPTER IX

## Buddha

The historical Buddha, as known to the custodians of the esoteric doctrine, is a personage whose birth is not invested with the quaint marvels popular story has crowded round it. Nor was his progress to adeptship traced by the literal occurrence of the super-natural struggles depicted in symbolic legend. On the other hand, the incarnation, which may outwardly be described as the birth of Buddha, is certainly not regarded by occult science as an event like any other birth, nor the spiritual development through which Buddha passed during his earth-life a mere process of intellectual evolution, like the mental history of any other philosopher. The mistake which ordinary European writers make in dealing with a problem of this sort, lies in their inclinations to treat exoteric legend either as a record of a miracle about which no more need be said, or as pure myth, putting merely a fantastic decoration on a remarkable life. This, it is assumed, however remarkable, must have been lived according to the theories of Nature at present accepted by the nineteenth century. The account which has now been given in the foregoing pages may prepare the way for a statement as to what the esoteric doctrine teaches concerning the real Buddha, who was born, as modern investigation has quite correctly ascertained, 643 years before the Christian era, at Kapila-Vastu, near Benares.

Exoteric conceptions, knowing nothing of the laws which govern the operations of Nature in her higher departments, can only explain an abnormal dignity attaching to some particular birth, by supposing that the physical body of the person concerned was generated in a miraculous manner. Hence the popular notion about Buddha, that his incarnation in this world was due to an immaculate conception. Occult science knows nothing of any process for the production of a physical human child other than that appointed by physical laws; but it does know a good deal concerning the limits within which the progressive "one life," or "spiritual monad," or continuous thread of a series of incarnations may select a definite child-bodies as their human tenements. By the operation of Karma, in the case of ordinary mankind, this selection is made, unconsciously as far as the antecedent spiritual Ego emerging from Devachan is concerned. But in those abnormal cases where the one life has already forced itself into the sixth principle - that is to say, where a man has become an adept, and has the power of guiding his own spiritual Ego, in full consciousness as to what he is about, after he has quitted the body in which he won adeptship, either temporarily or permanently - it is quite within his power to select his own next incarnation. During life, even, he gets above the Devachanic attraction. He becomes one of the conscious directing powers of the planetary system to which he belongs, and great as this mystery of selected re-incarnation may be, it is not by any means restricted to its application to such extraordinary events as the birth of a Buddha. It is a phenomenon frequently reproduced by the higher adepts to this day; and while a great deal recounted in popular Oriental mythology is either purely fictitious or entirely symbolical, the re-incarnations of the Dalai and Teshu Lamas of Tibet, at which travelers only laugh for want of the knowledge that might enable them to sift fact from fancy, is a sober, scientific achievement. In such cases the adept states beforehand in what child, when and where to be born, he is going to reincarnate, and he very rarely fails. We say very rarely, because there are some accidents of physical nature which cannot be entirely guarded against; and it is not absolutely certain that, with all the foresight even an adept may bring to bear upon the matter, the child he may choose to become - in his reincarnated state - may attain physical maturity successfully. And, meanwhile, *in the body*, the adept is relatively helpless. Out of the body he is just what he has been ever since he became an adept; but as regards the new body he has chosen to inhabit, he must let it grow up in the ordinary course of Nature, and educate it by ordinary processes, and initiate it by the regular occult method into adeptship, before he has got a body fully ready again for occult work on the physical plane. All these processes are immensely simplified, it is true, by the peculiar spiritual force working within; but at first, in the child's body, the adept soul is certainly cramped and embarrassed, and, as ordinary imagination might suggest, very uncomfortable and ill at ease. The situation would be very much misunderstood if the reader were to imagine that re-incarnation of the kind described is a privilege which adepts avail themselves of with pleasure.

Buddha's birth was a mystery of the kind described, and by the light of what has been said, it will be easy to go over the popular story of his miraculous origin, and trace the symbolic references to the facts of the situation in some even of the most grotesque fables. None, for example, can look less promising, as an allusion to anything like a scientific fact, than the statement that Buddha entered the side of his mother as a young white elephant. But the while elephant is simply the symbol of adeptship - something considered to be a rare and beautiful specimen of its kind. So with other ante-natal legends pointing to the fact that the future child's body had been chosen as the habitation of a great spirit already endowed with superlative wisdom and goodness. Indra and Brahma came to do homage to the child at his birth - that is to say, the powers of Nature were already in submission to the Spirit within him. The thirty-two signs of a Buddha, which legends describe by means of a ludicrous physical symbolism, are merely the various powers of adeptship.

The selection of the body known as Siddhartha, and afterwards as Gautama, son of Suddhodana, of Kapila-Vastu, as the human tenement of the enlightened human spirit, who had submitted to incarnation for the sake of teaching mankind, was *not* one of those rare failures spoken of above; on the contrary, it was a signally successful choice in all respects, and nothing interfered with the accomplishment of adeptship by the Buddha in his new body. The popular narrative of his ascetic struggles and temptations, and of his final attainment of Buddhahood under the Bo-tree, is nothing more, of course, than the exoteric version of his initiation.

From that period onward, his work was of a dual nature; he had to reform and revive the morals of the populace and the science of the adepts - for adeptship itself is subject to cyclic changes, and in need of periodical impulses. The explanation of this branch of the subject, in plain terms, will not alone be important for its own sake, but will be interesting to all students of exoteric Buddhism, as elucidating some of the puzzling complications of the more abstruse "Northern doctrine."

A Buddha visits the earth for each of the seven races of the great planetary period. The Buddha with whom we are occupied was the fourth of the series, and that is why he stands fourth in the list quoted by Mr Rhys Davids, from Burnouf - quoted as an illustration of the way the Northern doctrine has been, as Mr Davids supposes, inflated by metaphysical subtleties and absurdities crowded round the simple morality which sums up Buddhism as presented to the populace. The fifth, or Maitreya Buddha, will come after the final disappearance of the fifth race, and when the sixth race will already have been established on earth for some hundreds of thousands of years. The sixth will come at the beginning of the seventh race, and the seventh towards the close of that race.

This arrangement will seem, at the first glance, out of harmony with the general design of human evolution. Here we are, in the middle of the fifth race, and yet it is the fourth Buddha who has been identified with this race, and the fifth will not come till the fifth race is practically extinct. The explanation is to be found, however, in the great outlines of the esoteric cosmogony. At the beginning of each great planetary period, when obscuration comes to an end, and the human tide-wave in its progress round the chain of worlds arrives at the shore of a globe where no humanity has existed for milliards of years, a teacher is required from the first for the new crop of mankind about to spring up. Remember that the preliminary evolution of the mineral, vegetable, and animal kingdoms has been accomplished in preparation for the new round-period. With the first infusion of the life-current into the "missing link" species, the first race of the new series will begin to evolve. It is then that the Being, who may be considered the Buddha of the first race, appears. The Planetary Spirit, or Dhyan Chohan, who is - or, to avoid the suggestion of an erroneous idea by the use of a singular verb, let us defy grammar, and say, who are - Buddha in all his or their developments, incarnates among the young, innocent, teachable forerunners of the new humanity, and impresses the first broad principles of right and wrong, and the first truths of the esoteric doctrine on a sufficient number of receptive minds, to ensure the continued reverberation of the ideas so implanted through successive generations of men in the millions of years to come, before the first race shall have completed its course. It is this advent in the beginning of the roundperiod of a Divine Being in human form that starts the ineradicable conception of the anthropomorphic God in all exoteric religions.

The first Buddha of the series in which Gautama Buddha stands fourth, is thus the second incarnation of Avaloketiswara - the mystic name of the hosts of the Dhyan Chohans or Planetary Spirits belonging to our planetary chain - and though Gautama is thus the fourth incarnation of enlightenment by exoteric reckoning, he is really the fifth of the true series, and thus properly belonging to our fifth race.

Avaloketiswara, as just stated, is the mystic name of the hosts of the Dhyan Chohans; the proper meaning of the word is manifested wisdom, just as Addi-Buddha and Amitabha both mean abstract wisdom.

The doctrine, as quoted by Mr Davids, that "every earthly mortal Buddha has his pure and glorious counterpart in the mystic world, free from the debasing conditions of this material life - or, rather, that the Buddha under material conditions is only an appearance, the reflection, or emanation, or type of a Dhyani Buddha" - is perfectly correct; the number of Dhyani Buddhas, or Dhyan Chohans, or planetary spirits, perfected human spirits of former world-periods, is infinite, but only five are practically identified in exoteric, and seven in esoteric, teaching, and this identification, be it remembered, is a manner of speaking which must not be interpreted too literally, for there is a unity in the sublime spirit-life in question that leaves no room for the isolation of individuality. All this will be seen to harmonize perfectly with the revelations concerning Nature embodied in previous chapters, and need not, in any way, be attributed to mystic imaginings. The Dhyani Buddhas, or Dhyan Chohans, are the perfected humanity of previous manwantaric epochs, and their *collective intelligence* is described by the name "Addi Buddha," which Mr Rhys Davids is mistaken in treating as a comparatively recent invention of the Northern Buddhists. Addi- Buddha means primordial wisdom, and is mentioned in the oldest Sanscrit books. For example, in the philosophical dissertation on the "Mandukya Upanishad," by Gowdapatha, a Sanscrit author contemporary with Buddha himself, the expression is freely used and expounded in exact accordance with the present statement. A friend of mine in India, a Brahmin pundit of first-rate attainments as a Sanscrit scholar, has shown me a copy of this book, which has never yet, that he knows of, been translated into English, and has pointed out a sentence bearing on the present question, giving me the following translation: "Prakriti itself, in fact, is Addi-Buddha, and all the Dharmas have been existing from eternity." Gowdapatha is a philosophical writer respected by all Hindoo and Buddhist sects alike, and widely known. He was the guru, or spiritual teacher, of the first Sankaracharya, of whom I shall have to speak more at length very shortly.

Adeptship, when Buddha incarnated, was not the condensed, compact hierarchy that it has since become under his influence. There has never been an age of the world without its adepts; but they have sometimes been scattered throughout the world, they have sometimes been isolated in separate seclusions, they have gravitated now to this country, now to that; and finally, be it remembered, their knowledge and power has not always been inspired with the elevated and severe morality which Buddha infused into its latest and highest organization. The reform of the occult world by his instrumentality was, in fact, the result of his great sacrifice, of the self-denial which induced him to reject the blessed condition of Nirvana to which, after his earth-life as Buddha, he was fully entitled, and undertake the burden of renewed incarnations in order to carry out more thoroughly the task he had taken in hand, and confer a correspondingly increased benefit on mankind. Buddha re-incarnated himself, next after his existence as Gautama Buddha, in the person of the great teacher of whom but little is said in exoteric works on Buddhism, but without a consideration of whose life it would be impossible to get a correct conception of the position in the Eastern world of esoteric science - namely, Sankaracharya. The latter part of this name, it may be explained - acharya - merely means teacher. The whole name as a title is perpetuated to this day under curious circumstances, but the modern bearers of it are not in the direct line of Buddhist spiritual incarnations.

Sankaracharya appeared in India - no attention being paid to his birth, which appears to have taken place on the Malabar coast - about sixty years after Gautama Buddha's death - about sixty years after Gautama Buddha's death. Esoteric teaching is to the effect that Sankaracharya simply was Buddha in all respects, in a new body. This view will not be acceptable to the *uninitiated* Hindu authorities, who attribute a later date to Sankaracharya's appearance, and regard him as a wholly independent teacher, even inimical to Buddhism; but none the less is the statement just made the real opinion of *initiates* in esoteric science, whether these call themselves Buddhists or Hindus. I have received the information I am now giving from a Brahmin Adwaiti of Southern India - not directly from my Tibetan instructor - and all initiated Brahmins, he assures me, would say the same. Some of the later incarnations of Buddha are described differently as overshadowings by the spirit of Buddha, but in the person of Sankaracharya he reappeared on earth. The object he had in view was to fill up some gaps and repair certain errors in his own previous teaching; for there is no contention in esoteric Buddhism that even a Buddha can be absolutely infallible at every moment of his career.

The position was as follows: - Up to the time of Buddha, the Brahmins of India had jealously reserved occult knowledge as the appanage of their own caste. Exceptions were occasionally made in favour of Tshatryas, but the rule was exclusive in a very high degree. This rule Buddha broke down, admitting all castes equally to the path of adeptship. The change may have been perfectly right in principle, but it paved the way for a great deal of trouble, and, as the Brahmins conceived, for the degradation of occult knowledge itself - that is to say, its transfer to unworthy hands, not unworthy merely because of caste inferiority, but because of the moral inferiority which they conceived to be introduced into the occult fraternity together with brothers of low birth. The Brahmin contention would not by any means be, that because a man should be a Brahmin, it followed that he was necessarily virtuous and trustworthy; but the argument would be: It is supremely necessary to keep out all but the virtuous and trustworthy from the secrets and powers of initiation. To that end it is necessary not only to set up all the ordeals, probations, and tests we can think of, but also to take no candidates except from the class which, on the whole, by reason of its hereditary advantages, is likely to be the best nursery of fit candidates.

Later experience is held on all hands now to have gone far towards vindicating the Brahmin apprehension, and the next incarnation of Buddha, after that in the person of Sankaracharya, was a practical admission of this; but meanwhile, in the person of Sankaracharya, Buddha was engaged in smoothing over, beforehand, the sectarian strife in India which he saw impending. The active opposition of the Brahmins against Buddhism began in Asoka's time, when the great efforts made by that ruler to spread Buddhism provoked an apprehension on their part in reference to their social and political ascendency. It must be remembered that initiates are not wholly free in all cases from the prejudices of their own individualities. They possess *some* such god-like attributes that outsiders, when they first begin to understand something of these, are apt to divest them, in imagination, even too completely of human frailties. Initiation and occult knowledge, held in common, is certainly a bond of union, among adepts of all nationalities, which is far stronger than any other bond. But it has been found on more occasions than one to fail in obliterating all other distinctions. Thus the Buddhist and Brahmin initiates of the period referred to were by no means of one mind on all questions, and the Brahmins very decidedly disapproved of the Buddhist reformation in its exoteric aspects. Chandragupta, Asoka's grandfather, was an upstart, and the family were Sudras. This was enough to render his Buddhist policy unattractive to the representatives of the orthodox Brahmin faith. The struggle assumed a very embittered form, though ordinary history gives us few or no particulars. The party of primitive Buddhism was entirely worsted, and the Brahmin ascendency completely re-established in the time of Vikramaditya, about 80 B.C. But Sankaracharya had traveled all over India in advance of the great struggle, and had established various *mathams*, or schools of philosophy, in several important centres. He was only engaged in this task for a few years, but the influence of his teaching has been so stupendous that its very magnitude disguises the change wrought. He brought exoteric Hinduism into practical harmony with the esoteric "wisdom religion," and left the people amusing themselves still with their ancient mythologies, but leaning on philosophical guides who were esoteric Buddhists to all intents and purposes, though in reconciliation with all that was ineradicable in Brahminism. The great fault of previous exoteric Hinduism lay in its attachment to vain ceremonial, and its adhesion to idolatrous conceptions of the divinities of the Hindu Pantheon. Sankaracharya emphasized, by his commentaries on the Upanishads, and by his original writings, the necessity of pursuing *gnyanam* in order to obtain *moksha* - that is to say, the importance of the secret knowledge, to spiritual progress and the consummation thereof. He was the founder of the Vedantin system - the proper meaning of Vedanta being the final end or crown of knowledge - though the sanctions of that system are derived by him from the writings of Vyasa, the author of the "Mahabharata," the "Puranas," and the "Brahmasutras." I make these statements, the reader will understand, not on the basis of any researches of my own - which I am not Oriental scholar enough to attempt - but on the authority of a Brahmin initiate who is himself a first-rate Sanscrit scholar as well as an occultist.

The Vedantin school at present is almost co-extensive with Hinduism, making allowance, of course, for the existence of some special sects, like the Sikhs, the Vallabacharyas, or Maharajah sect, of very unfair fame, and may be divided into three great divisions - the Adwaitees, the Vishishta Adwaitees, and the Dwaitees. The outline of the Adwaitee doctrine is that *brahmum* or *purush*, the universal spirit, acts only through *prakriti*, matter, that everything takes place in this way through the inherent energy of matter. Brahmum, or Parabrahm, is thus a passive, incomprehensible, unconscious principle, but the essence, one life, or energy of the universe. In this way the doctrine is identical with the transcendental materialism of the adept esoteric Buddhist philosophy. The name Adwaitee signifies *not dual*, and has reference partly to the non-duality, or unity of the universal spirit, or Buddhist one life, as distinguished from the notion of its operation through anthropomorphic emanations; partly to the unity of the universal and the human spirit. As a natural consequence of this doctrine, the Adwaitees infer the Buddhist doctrine of Karma, regarding the future destiny of man, as altogether depending on the causes he himself engenders.

The Vishishta Adwaitees modify these views by the interpolation of Vishnu as a conscious deity, the primary emanation of Parabrahm, Vishu being regarded as a personal god, capable of intervening in the course of human destiny. They do not regard *yog*, or spiritual training, as the proper avenue to spiritual achievement, but conceive this to be possible, chiefly by means of *Bhakti*, or devoutness. Roughly stated in the phraseology of European theology, the Adwaitee may thus be said to believe only in salvation by works, the Vishishta Adwaitee in salvation by grace. The Dwaitee differs but little from the Vishishta Adwaitee, merely affirming, by the designation he assumes, with increased emphasis the duality of the human spirit and the highest principle of the universe, and including many ceremonial observances as an essential part of *Bhakti*.

But all these differences of view, it must be borne in mind, have to do merely with the exoteric variations on the fundamental idea, introduced by different teachers with varying impressions as to the capacity of the populace for assimilating transcendental ideas. All leaders of Vedantin thought look up to Sankaracharva and the mathams he established with the greatest possible reverence, and their inner faith runs up in all cases into the one esoteric doctrine. In fact the initiates of all schools in India interlace with one another. Except as regards nomenclature, the whole system of cosmogony, as held by the Buddhist-Arhats, and as set forth in this volume, is equally held by initiated Brahmins, and has been equally held by them since before Buddha's birth. Whence did they obtain it? the reader may ask. Their answer would be from the Planetary Spirit, or Dhyan Chohan, who first visited this planet at the dawn of the human race in the present round-period - more millions of years ago than I like to mention on the basis of conjecture, while the real exact number is withheld.

Sankaracharya founded four principal mathams, one at Sringari, in Southern India, which has always remained the most important; one at Juggernath, in Orissa; one at Dwaraka, in Kathiawar; and one at Gungotri, on the slopes of the Himalayas in the North. The chief of the Sringari temple has always borne the designation Sankaracharya, in addition to some individual name. From these four centres others have been established, and mathams now exist all over India, exercising the utmost possible influence on Hinduism.

I have said that Buddha, by his third incarnation, recognized the fact that he had, in the excessive confidence of his loving trust in the perfectibility of humanity, opened the doors of the occult sanctuary too widely. His third appearance was in the person of Tsong-ka-pa, the great Tibetan adept reformer of the fourteenth century. In this personality he was exclusively concerned with the affairs of the adept fraternity, by that time collecting chiefly in Tibet.

From time immemorial there had been a certain secret region in Tibet, which to this day is quite unknown to and unapproachable by any but initiated persons, and inaccessible to the ordinary people of the country as to any others, in which adepts have always congregated. But the country generally was not in Buddha's time, as it has since become, the chosen habitation of the great brotherhood. Much more than they are at present, were the Mahatmas in former times, distributed about the world. The progress of civilization, engendering the magnetism they find so trying, had, however, by the date with which we are now dealing - the fourteenth century - already given rise to a very general movement towards Tibet on the part of the previously dissociated occultists. Far more widely than was held to be consistent with the safety of mankind was occult knowledge and power then found to be disseminated. To the task of putting it under the control of a rigid system of rule and law did Tsong-ka-pa address himself.

Without re-establishing the system on the previous unreasonable basis of caste exclusiveness, he elaborated a code of rules for the guidance of the adepts, the effect of which was to weed out of the occult body all but those who sought occult knowledge in a spirit of the most sublime devotion to the highest moral principles.

An article in the Theosophist for March, 1882, on "Re-incarnations in Tibet," for the complete trustworthiness of which in all its mystic bearings I have the highest assurance, gives a great deal of important information about the branch of the subject with which we are now engaged, and the relations between esoteric Buddhism and Tibet, which cannot be examined too closely by any one who desires an exhaustive comprehension of Buddhism in its real signification.

"The regular system," we read, "of the Lamaic incarnations of 'Sangyas' (or Buddha) began with Tsongkha- pa. This reformer is not the incarnation of one of the five celestial Dhyanis or heavenly Buddhas, as is generally supposed, said to have been created by Sakya Muni after he had risen to Nirvana, but that of Amita, one of the Chinese names for Buddha. The records preserved in the Gon-pa (lamasery) of Tdashi Hlum-po (spelt by the English *Teshu Lumbo*) show that Sangyas incarnated himself in Tsong-kha-pa in consequence of the great degradation his doctrines had fallen into. Until then there had been no other incarnations than those of the five celestial Buddhas, and of their Boddhisatvas, each of the former having created (read, overshadowed with his spiritual wisdom) five of the last named . . . . . It was because, among many other reforms, Tsong-kha-pa forbade necromancy (which is practiced to this day with the most disgusting rites by the Bhons - the aborigines of Tibet, with whom the Red Caps or Shammars had always fraternized) that the latter resisted his authority. This act was followed by a split between the two sects. Separating entirely from the Gyalukpas, the Dugpas (Red Caps), from the first in a great minority, settled in various parts of Tibet, chiefly its border-lands, and principally in Nepaul and Bhootan. But, while they retained a sort of independence at the monastery of Sakia-Djong, the Tibetan residence of their spiritual (?) chief, Gong-sso Rimbo-chay, the Bhootanese have been from their beginning the tributaries and vassals of the Dalai Lamas.

"The Tda-shi Lamas were always more powerful and more highly considered than the Dalai Lamas. The latter are the creation of the Tda-shi Lama, Nabang-lob-sang, the sixth incarnation of Tsong-kha-pa, himself an incarnation of Amitabha or Buddha."

Several writers on Buddhism have entertained a theory, which Mr Clements Markham formulates very fully in his "Narrative of the Mission of George Bogle to Tibet," that whereas the original Scriptures of Buddhism were taken to Ceylon by the son of Asoka, the Buddhism which found its way into Tibet from India and China was gradually overlaid with a mass of dogma and metaphysical speculation. And Professor Max Müller says: - "The most important element in the Buddhist reform has always been its social and moral code, not its metaphysical theories. That moral code, taken by itself, is one of the most perfect which the world has ever known; and it was this blessing that the introduction of Buddhism brought into Tibet."

"The blessing," says the authoritative article in the Theosophist, from which I have just been quoting, "has remained and spread all over the country, there being no kinder, purer-minded, more simple, or sinfearing nation than the Tibetans. But for all that, the popular lamaism, when compared with the real esoteric, or Arahat, Buddhism of Tibet, offers a contrast as great at the snow trodden along a road in the valley to the pure and undefiled mass which glitters on the top of a high mountain peak."

The fact is, that Ceylon is saturated with exoteric, and Tibet with esoteric, Buddhism. Ceylon concerns itself merely or mainly with the morals, Tibet, or rather the adepts of Tibet, with the science, of Buddhism.

These explanations constitute but a sketch of the whole position. I do not possess the arguments nor the literary leisure which would be required for its amplification into a finished picture of the relations which really subsist between the inner principles of Hinduism and those of Buddhism. And I am quite alive to the possibility that many learned and painstaking students of the subject will have formed, as the consequences of prolonged and erudite research, conclusions with which the explanations I am now enabled to give, may seem at first sight to conflict. But none the less are these explanations directly gathered from authorities to whom the subject is no less familiar in its scholarly than in its esoteric aspect. And their inner knowledge throws a light upon the whole position which wholly exempts them from the danger of misconstruing texts and mistaking the bearings of obscure symbology. To know when Gautama Buddha was born, what is recorded of his teaching, and what popular legends have gathered round his biography, is to know next to nothing of the real Buddha, so much greater than either the historical moral teacher, or the fantastic demigod of tradition. And it is only when we have comprehended the link between Buddhism and Brahaminism that the greatness of the esoteric doctrine rises into its true proportions.

# CHAPTER X

## Nirvana

A complete assimilation of esoteric teaching up to the point we have now reached will enable us to approach the consideration of the subject which exoteric writers on Buddhism have generally treated as the doctrinal starting-point of that religion.

Hitherto, for want of any better method of seeking out the true meaning of Nirvana, Buddhist scholars have generally picked the world to pieces, and examined its roots and fragments. One might as hopefully seek to ascertain the smell of a flower by dissecting the paper on which its picture was painted. It is difficult for minds schooled in the intellectual processes of physical research - as all our Western nineteenth-century minds are, directly or indirectly - to comprehend the first spiritual state above this life, that of Devachan. Such conditions of existence are but partly for the understanding, a higher faculty must be employed to realize them, and all the more is it possible to force their meaning upon another mind by words. It is by first awakening that higher faculty in his pupil, and then putting the pupil in a position to observe for himself, that the regular occult teacher proceeds in such a matter.

Now there are the usual *seven* states of Devachan, suited to the different degrees of spiritual enlightenment which the various candidates for that condition may obtain; there are *rupa* and *arupa locas* in Devachan - that is to say, states which take (subjective) consciousness of form and states which transcend these again. And yet the highest Devachanic state in *arupa loca* is not to be compared to that wonderful condition of pure spirituality which is spoken of as Nirvana.

In the ordinary course of Nature during a round, when the spiritual monad has accomplished the tremendous journey from the first planet to the seventh, and has finished for the time being its existence there - finished all its multifarious existences there, with their respective periods of Devachan between each - the Ego passes into a spiritual condition, different from the Devachanic state, in which, for periods of inconceivable duration, it rests before resuming its circuit of the worlds. That condition may be regarded as the Devachan of its Devachanic states - a sort of review thereof - a superior state to those reviewed, just as the Devachanic state belonging to any one existence on earth is a superior state to that of the half-developed spiritual aspirations or impulses of affection of the earth-life. That period - that intercyclic period of extraordinary exaltation, as compared to any that have gone before, as compared even with the subjective conditions of the planets in the ascending arc, so greatly superior to our own as these are - is spoken of in esoteric science as a state of partial Nirvana. Carrying on imagination through immeasurable vistas of the future, we must next conceive ourselves approaching the period which would correspond to the intercyclic period of the seventh round of humanity, in which men have become as gods. The very last, most elevated, and glorious of the objective lives having been completed, the perfected spiritual being reaches a condition in which a complete recollection of all lives lived at any time in the past returns to him. He can look back over the curious masquerade of objective existences, as it will seem to him then, over the minutest details of any of these earth-lives among the number through which he has passed, and can cognizance of them and of all things with which they were in any way associated, for in regard to this planetary chain he has reached omniscience. This supreme development of individuality is the great reward which Nature reserves not only for those who secure it prematurely, so to speak, by the relatively brief, but desperate and terrible struggles which lead to adeptship, but also for all who, by the distinct preponderance of good over evil in the character of the whole series of their incarnations, have passed through the valley of the shadow of death in the middle of the fifth round, and have worked their way up to it in the sixth and seventh rounds.

This sublimely blessed state is spoken of in esoteric science as the threshold of Nirvana.

Is it worth while to go any further in speculation as to what follows? One may be told that no state of individual consciousness, even though but a phase of feeling already identified in a large measure with the general consciousness on that level of existence, can be equal in spiritual elevation to absolute consciousness in which all sense of individuality is merged in the whole. We may use such phrases as intellectual counters, but for no ordinary mind - dominated by its physical brain and brain-born intellect - can they have a living signification.

All that words can convey is that Nirvana is a sublime state of conscious rest in omniscience. It would be ludicrous, after all that has gone before, to turn to the various discussions which have been carried on by students of exoteric Buddhism as to whether Nirvana does or does not mean annihilation. Worldly similes fall short of indicating the feeling with which the graduates of esoteric science regard such a question. Does the last penalty of the law mean the highest honour of the peerage? Is a wooden spoon the emblem of the most illustrious pre-eminence in learning? Such questions as these but faintly symbolize the extravagance of the question whether Nirvana is held by Buddhism to be equivalent to annihilation. And in some, to us inconceivable, way the state of para-Nirvana is spoken of as immeasurably higher than that of Nirvana. I do not pretend myself to attach any meaning to the statement, but it may serve to show what a very transcendental realm of thought the subject belongs.

A great deal of confusion of mind respecting Nirvana has arisen from statements made concerning Buddha. He is said to have attained Nirvana while on earth; he is also said to have foregone Nirvana, in order to submit to renewed incarnations for the good of humanity. The two statements are quite reconcilable.

As a *great* adept, Buddha naturally attained to that which is the great achievement of adeptship on earth, - the passing of his own Ego-spirit into the ineffable condition of Nirvana. Let it not be supposed that for any adept such a passage is one that can be lightly undertaken. Only stray hints about the nature of this great mystery have reached me, but, putting these together, I believe I am right in saying that the achievement in question is one which only some of the high initiates are qualified to attempt, which exacts a total suspension of animation in the body for periods of time compared to which the longest cataleptic trances known to ordinary science are insignificant, the protection of the physical frame from natural decay during this period by means which the resources of occult science are strained to accomplish; and withal it is a process involving a double risk to the continued earthly life of the person who undertakes it. One of these risks is the doubt whether, when once Nirvana is attained, the Ego will be willing to return. That the return will be a terrible effort and sacrifice is certain, and will only be prompted by the most devoted attachment, on the part of the spiritual traveler, to the idea of duty in its purest abstraction. The second great risk is that allowing the sense of duty to predominate over the temptation to stay, a temptation, be it remembered, that is not weakened by the notion that any conceivable penalty can attach to it - even then it is always doubtful whether the traveler will be able to return. In spite of all this, however, there have been many other adepts besides Buddha who have made the great passage, and for whom those about them at such times have said the return to their prison of ignoble flesh, - though so noble *ex hypothesi* compared to most such tenements, - has left them paralyzed with depression for weeks. To begin the weary round of physical life again, to stoop to earth after having been in Nirvana, is too dreadful a collapse.

Buddha's renunciation was in some inexplicable manner greater again, because he not merely returned from Nirvana for duty's sake, to finish the earth-life in which he was engaged as Gautama Buddha, but when all the claims of duty had been fully satisfied, and his right of passage into Nirvana for incalculable aeons entirely earned under the most enlarged view of his earthly mission, he gave up that reward, or rather postponed it for an indefinite period, to undertake a supererogatory series of incarnations for the sake of humanity at large. How is humanity being benefited by this renunciation? it may be asked. But the question can only be suggested in reality by that deep-seated habit, we have most of us acquired, of estimating benefit by a physical standard, and even in regard to this standard of taking very short views of human affairs. No one will have followed me through the foregoing chapter on the Progress of Humanity without perceiving what kind of benefit it would be that Buddha would wish to confer on men. That which is necessarily for him the great question in regard to humanity, is how to help as many people as possible across the great critical period of the fifth round.

Until that time everything is a mere preparation for the supreme struggle, in the estimation of an adept, all the more of a Buddha. The material welfare of the existing generation is not even as dust in the balance of such a calculation; the only thing of importance at present is, to cultivate those tendencies in mankind which may launch as many Egos as possible upon such a Karmic path that the growth of their spirituality in future births will be promoted. Certainly it is the fixed conviction of esoteric teachers - of the adept coworkers with Buddha - that the very process of cultivating such spirituality will immensely reduce the sum of even transitory human sorrow. And the happiness of mankind, even in any one generation only, is by no means a matter on which esoteric science looks with indifference. So the esoteric policy is not to be considered as something so hopelessly up in the air that it will never concern any of us who are living now. But there are seasons of good and bad harvest for wheat and barley, and so also for the desired growth of spirituality amongst men; and in Europe, at all events, going by the experience of former great races, at periods of development corresponding to that of our own now, the great present uprush of intelligence in the direction of physical and material progress is not likely to bring on a season of good harvests for progress of the other kind. For the moment the best chance of doing good in countries where the uprush referred to is most marked, is held to lie in the possibility that the importance of spirituality may come to be perceived by intellect, even in advance of being felt, if the attention of that keen though unsympathetic tribunal can but be secured. Any success in that direction to which these explanations may conduce, will justify the views of those - but a minority - among the esoteric guardians of humanity who have conceived that it is worth while to have them made.

So Nirvana is truly the key-note of esoteric Buddhism, as of the hitherto rather misdirected studies of external scholars. The great end of the whole stupendous evolution of humanity is to cultivate human souls so that they shall be ultimately fit for that as yet inconceivable condition. The great triumph of the present race of planetary spirits who have reached that condition themselves, will be to draw thither as many more Egos as possible. We are far as yet from the era at which we may be in serious danger of disqualifying ourselves definitively for such progress, but it is not too soon even now to begin the great process of qualification, all the more as the Karma which will propagate itself through successive lives in that direction will carry its own reward with it, so that an enlightened pursuit of our highest interests, in the very remote future, will coincide with the pursuit of our immediate welfare in the next Devachanic period, and the next rebirth.

Will it be argued that if the cultivation of spirituality is the great purpose to be followed, it matters little whether men pursue it along one religious pathway or another? This is a mistake which, as explained in a former chapter, Buddha, as Sankaracharya, set himself especially to combat - viz the early Hindu belief that *moksha* can be attained by *bhakti* irrespective of *gnyanam* - that is, that salvation is obtainable by devout practices irrespective of knowledge of eternal truth. The sort of salvation we are talking about now is not escape from a penalty, to be achieved by cajoling a celestial potentate - it is a positive and not a negative achievement - the ascent into regions of spiritual elevation so exalted that the candidate aiming at them is claiming that which we ordinarily describe as omniscience. Surely it is plain, from the way Nature habitually works, that under no circumstances will a time ever come when a person, merely by reason of having been good, will suddenly become wise. The supreme goodness *and wisdom* of the sixth-round man, who, once becoming that, will assimilate by degrees the attributes of divinity itself, can only be grown by degrees themselves, and goodness alone, associated, as we so often find it, with the most grotesque religious beliefs, cannot conduct a man to more than Devachanic periods of devout but unintelligent rapture, and in the end, if similar conditions are reproduced through many existences, to some painless extinction of individuality at the great crisis.

It is by a steady pursuit of, and desire for, real spiritual truth, not by an idle, however well-meaning acquiescence in the fashionable dogmas of the nearest church, that men launch their souls into the subjective state, prepared to imbibe real knowledge from the latent omniscience of their own sixth principles, and to re-incarnate in due time with impulses in the same direction. Nothing can produce more disastrous effects on human progress, as regards the destiny of individuals, than the very prevalent notion that one religion followed out in a pious spirit, is as good as another, and that if such and such doctrines are perhaps absurd when you look into them, the great majority of good people will never think of their absurdity, but will recite them in a blamelessly devoted attitude of mind. One religion is by no means as good as another, even if all were productive of equally blameless lives. But I prefer to avoid all criticism of specific faiths, leaving this volume a simple and inoffensive statement of the real inner doctrines of the one great religion of the world which -presenting as it does in its external aspects a bloodless and innocent record - has thus been really productive of blameless lives throughout its whole existence. Moreover, it would not be by a servile acceptance even if its doctrines that the development of true spirituality is to be cultivated. It is by the disposition to seek truth, to test and examine all which presents itself as claiming belief, that the great result is to be brought about. In the East, such a resolution in the highest degree leads to chelaship, to the pursuit of truth, knowledge, by the development of inner faculties by means of which it may be cognized with certainty. In the west, the realm of intellect, as the world is mapped out at present, truth unfortunately can only be pursued and hunted out with the help of many words and much wrangling and disputation. But at all events it may be hunted, and, if it is not finally captured, the chase on the part of the hunters will have engendered instincts that will propagate themselves and lead to results hereafter.

# CHAPTER XI

## The Universe

In all Oriental literature bearing on the constitution of the cosmos, frequent reference is made to the days and the nights of ; the in-breathings and the out-breathings of the creative principle, the periods of manvantara, [As transliterated into English, this word may be written either *manwantara* or *manvantara*; and the proper pronunciation is something between the two, with the accent on the second syllable.] and the periods of pralaya. This idea runs into various Eastern mythologies, but in its symbolical aspects we need not follow it here. The process in Nature to which it refers is of course the alternate succession of activity and repose that is observable at every step of the great ascent from the infinitely small to the infinitely great. Man has a manvantara and pralaya every four-and-twenty hours, his periods of waking and sleeping; vegetation follows the same rule from year to year as it subsides and revives with the seasons. The world, too, has its manvantaras and pralayas, when the tide-wave of humanity approaches its shore, runs through the evolution of its seven races, and ebbs away again, and such a manvantara has been treated by most exoteric religions as the whole cycle of eternity.

The major manvantara of our planetary chain is that which comes to an end when the last Dhyan Chohan of the seventh round of perfected humanity passes into Nirvana. And the expression has thus to be regarded as one of considerable elasticity. It may be said indeed to have infinite elasticity, and that is one explanation of the confusion which has reigned in all treatises on Eastern religions in their popular aspects. All the root-words transferred to popular literature from the secret doctrine have a seven-fold significance at least, for the initiate, while the uninitiated reader, naturally supposing that one word means one thing, and trying always to clear up its meaning by collating its various applications, and striking an average, gets into the most hopeless embarrassment.

The planetary chain with which we are concerned is not the only one which has our sun as its centre. As there are other planets besides the earth in our chain, so there are other chains besides this in our solar system. There are seven such, and there comes a time when all these go into pralaya together. This is spoken of as solar pralaya, and within the interval between two such pralayas, the vast solar manvantara covers seven pralayas and manvantaras of our - and each other - planetary chain. Thought is baffled, say even the adepts, in speculating as to how many of our solar pralayas must come before the great cosmic night in which the whole universe, in its collective enormity, obeys what is manifestly the universal law of activity and repose, and with all its myriad systems passes itself into pralaya. But even that tremendous result, says esoteric science, must surely come.

After the pralaya of a single planetary chain there is no necessity for a recommencement of evolutionary activity absolutely *de novo*. There is only a resumption of arrested activity. The vegetable and animal kingdoms, which at the end of the last corresponding manvantara had reached only a partial development, are not destroyed. Their life or vital energy passes through a night, or period of rest; they also have, so to speak, a Nirvana of their own, as why should they not, these foetal and infant entities? They are all, like ourselves, begotten of the one element. As we have our Dhyan Chohans, so have they in their several kingdoms elemental guardians, and are as well taken care of in the mass as humanity is in the mass. The one element not only fills and *is* space, but interpenetrates every atom of cosmic matter.

When, however, the hour of the solar pralaya strikes, though the process of man's advance on his last seventh round is precisely the same as usual, each planet, instead of merely passing out of the visible into the invisible, as he quits it in turn, is annihilated. With the beginning of the seventh round of the seventh planetary chain manvantara, every kingdom having now reached its last cycle, there remains on each planet, after the exit of man, merely the *maya* of once living and existing forms. With every step he takes on the descending and ascending arcs, as he moves on from globe to globe, the planet left behind becomes an empty chrysaloidal case. At his departure there is an outflow from every kingdom of its entities. Waiting to pass into higher forms in due time, they are nevertheless liberated, and to the day of the next evolution they will rest in their lethargic sleep in space, until brought into life again at the new solar manvantara. The old elementals will rest till they are called on to become in their turn the bodies of mineral, vegetable, and animal entities on another and a higher chain of globes on their way to become human entities, while the germinal entities of the lowest forms - and at that time there will remain but few of such - will hang in space like drops of water suddenly turned into icicles. They will thaw at the first hot breath of the new solar manvantara, and form the soul of the future globes. The slow development of the vegetable kingdom, up to the period we are now dealing with, will have been provided for by the longer interplanetary rest of man. When the solar pralaya comes, the whole purified humanity merges into Nirvana, and from that intersolar Nirvana will be reborn in the higher systems. The strings of worlds are destroyed, and vanish like a shadow from the wall when the light is extinguished. "We have every indication," say the adepts, "that at this very moment such a solar pralaya is taking place, while there are two minor ones ending somewhere."

At the beginning of the new solar manvantara the hitherto subjective elements of the material worlds, now scattered in cosmic dust, receiving their impulse from the new Dhyan Chohans of the new solar system (the highest of the old ones having gone higher), will form into primordial ripples of life, and, separating into differentiating centres of activity, combine in a graduated scale of seven stages of evolution. Like every other orb of space, our earth has, before obtaining its ultimate materiality, to pass through a gamut of seven stages of density. Nothing in this world now can give us an idea of what that ultimate stage of materiality is like. The French astronomer Flammarion, in a book called *La Resurrection et la Fin des Mondes*, has approached a conception of this ultimate materiality. The facts are, I am informed, with slight modifications, much as he surmises. In consequence of what he treats as secular refrigeration, but which more truly is old age and loss of vital power, the solidification and desication of the earth at last reaches a point when the whole globe becomes a relaxed conglomerate. Its period of child-bearing has gone by; its progeny are all nurtured; its term of life is finished. Hence its constituent masses cease to obey those laws of cohesion and aggregation which held them together. And becoming like a corpse, which, abandoned to the work of destruction, leaves each molecule composing it free to separate itself from the body, and obey in future the sway of new influences, "the attraction of the moon," suggests M. Flammarion, "would itself undertake the task of demolition by producing a tidal wave of earth particles instead of an aqueous tide." This last idea must not be regarded as countenanced by occult science except so far as it may serve to illustrate the loss of molecular cohesion in the material of the earth.

Occult physics pass fairly into the region of metaphysics, if we seek to obtain some indication of the way in which evolution recommences after a universal pralaya.

The one eternal, imperishable thing in the universe, which universal pralayas themselves pass over without destroying, is that which may be regarded indifferently as space, duration, matter or motion; not as something having these four attributes, but as something which is these four things at once and always. And evolution takes its rise in the atomic polarity which motion engenders. In cosmogony the positive and the negative, or the active and the passive, forces correspond to the male and female principles. The spiritual efflux enters into the veil of cosmic matter; the active is attracted by the passive principle, and if we may here assist imagination by having recourse to old occult symbology - the great Nag - the serpent emblem of eternity, attracts its tail to its mouth, forming thereby the circle of eternity, or rather cycles in eternity. The one and chief attribute of the universal spiritual principle, the unconscious but ever active life-giver, is to expand and shed; that of the universal material principle is to gather in and fecundate. Unconscious and non-existing when separate, they become consciousness and life when brought together. The word Brahma comes from the Sanscrit root *brih*, to expand, grow, or fructify, esoteric cosmogony being but the vivifying expansive force of Nature in its eternal evolution. No one expression can have contributed more to mislead the human mind in basic speculation concerning the origin of things than the word "creation." Talk of creation, and we are continually butting against the facts. But once realize that our planet and ourselves are no more creations than an iceberg, but states of being for a given time - that their present appearance, geological or anthropological, is transitory and but a condition concomitant of that stage of evolution at which they have arrived - and the way has been prepared for correct thinking. Then we are enabled to see what is meant by the one and only principle or element in the universe, and by the treatment of that element as androgynous; also by the proclamation of Hindu philosophy that all things are but Maya - transitory states - except the one element which rests during the maha-pralayas only - the nights of Brahma.

Perhaps we have now plunged deeply enough into the fathomless mystery of the great First Cause. It is no paradox to say that, simply by reason of ignorance, do ordinary theologians think they know so much about God. And it is no exaggeration to say that the wondrously endowed representatives of occult science, whose mortal nature has been so far elevated and purified that their perceptions range over other worlds and other states of existence, and commune directly with beings as much greater than ordinary mankind, as man is greater than the insects of the field, it is the mere truth that they never occupy themselves at all with any conception remotely resembling the God of churches and creeds. Within the limits of the solar system, the mortal adept knows, of his own knowledge, that all things are accounted for by the law, working on matter in its diverse forms, *plus* the guiding and modifying influence of the highest intelligences associated with the solar system, the Dhyan Chohans, the perfected humanity of the last preceding manvantara. These Dhyan Chohans, or Planetary Spirits, on whose nature it is almost fruitless to ponder, until one can at least realize the nature of disembodied existence in one's own case, impart to the reawakening worlds at the end of a planetary chain pralaya such impulses that evolution feels them throughout its whole progress. The limits of Nature's great law restrain their action. They cannot say, let there be paradise throughout space, let all men be born supremely wise and good; they can only work through the principle of evolution, and they cannot deny to any man who is to be invested with the potentiality of development himself into a Dhyan Chohan, the right to do evil, if he prefers that to good. Nor can they prevent evil, if done, from producing suffering. Objective life is the soil in which the life-germs are planted; spiritual existence (the expression being used, remember, in contrast merely to grossly material existence) is the flower to be ultimately obtained. But the human germ is something more than a flower seed; it has liberty of choice in regard to growing up or growing down, and it could not be developed without such liberty being exercised by the plant. This is the necessity of evil. But within the limits that logical necessity prescribes, the Dhyan Chohan impresses his conceptions upon the evolutionary tide, and comprehends the origin of all that he beholds.

Surely as we ponder in this way over the magnitude of the cyclic evolution with which esoteric science is in this way engaged, it seems reasonable to postpone considerations as to the origin of the whole cosmos. The ordinary man in this earth-life, with many, certainly some hundred, earth-lives to come, and their very much more important inter-incarnation periods (more important, that is, as regards duration and the prospect of happiness or sorrow) also in prospect, may surely be most wisely occupied with the inquiries whose issue will affect practical results, than with speculation in which he is practically quite uninterested. Of course, from the point of view of religious speculation resting on no positive knowledge of anything beyond this life, nothing can be more important or more highly practical than conjectures as to the attributes and probable intentions of the terrible, personal Jehovah, pictured as an omnipotent tribunal, into whose presence the soul at its death is to be introduced for judgement. But scientific knowledge of spiritual things throws back the day of judgement into a very dim perspective, the intervening period being filled with activity of all kinds. Moreover, it shows mankind that certainly, for millions and millions of centuries to come, it will not be confronted with any judge at all, other than that all-pervading judge, that Seventh Principle, or Universal Spirit, which exists everywhere, and, operating on matter, provokes the existence of man himself, and the world in which he lives, and the future conditions towards which he is pressing. The Seventh Principle, undefinable, incomprehensible for us at our present stage of enlightenment, is of course the only God recognized by esoteric knowledge, and no personification of this can be otherwise than symbolical.

And yet, in truth, esoteric knowledge, giving life and reality to ancient symbolism in one direction, as often as it conflicts with modern dogma in the other, shows how far from absolutely fabulous are even the most anthropomorphic notions of Deity associated by exoteric tradition with the beginning of the world. The Planetary Spirit, actually incarnated among men in the first round, was the prototype of personal deity in all subsequent developments of the idea. The mistake made by uninstructed men in dealing with the idea is merely one of degree. The personal God of an insignificant minor manvantara has been taken for the creator of the whole cosmos, a most natural mistake for people forced, by knowing no more of human destiny than was included in one objective incarnation, to suppose that all beyond was a homogeneous spiritual future. The God of this life, of course, for them, was the God of all lives and worlds and periods.

The reader will not misunderstand me, I trust, to mean that esoteric science regards the Planetary Spirit of the first round as a god. As I say, it is concerned with the working of Nature in an immeasurable space, from an immeasurable past, and all through immeasurable future. The enormous areas of time and space in which our solar system operates *is* explorable by the mortal adepts of esoteric science. Within those limits they know all that takes place, and how it takes place, and they know that everything is accounted for by the constructive will of the collective host of the Planetary Spirits, operating under the law of evolution that pervades all Nature. They commune with these Planetary Spirits, and learn from them that the law of this, is the law of other solar systems as well, into the regions of which the perceptive faculties of the Planetary Spirits can plunge as the perceptive faculties of the adepts themselves can plunge into the life of other planets of this chain. The law of alternating activity and repose is operating universally; for the whole cosmos, even though at unthinkable intervals, pralaya must succeed manvantara, and manvantara, pralaya.

Will any one ask to what end does this eternal succession work? Is it better to confine the question to a single system, and as to what end does the original nebula arrange itself in planetary vortices of evolution, and develop worlds in which the universal spirit, reverberating through matter, produces form and life and those higher states of matter in which that which we call subjective or spiritual existence is provided for. Surely it is end enough to satisfy any reasonable mind that such sublimely perfected beings as the Planetary Spirits themselves come thus into existence, and live a conscious life of supreme knowledge and felicity, through vistas of time which are equivalent to all we can imagine of eternity. Into this unutterable greatness every living thing has the opportunity of passing ultimately. The Spirit which is in every animated form, and which has even worked up into these, from forms we are generally in the habit of calling inanimate, will slowly but certainly progress onwards until the working of its untiring influence in matter has evolved a human soul. It does not follow that the plants and animals around us have any principle evolved in them as yet which will assume a human form in the course of the present manvantara; but though the course of an incomplete evolution may be suspended by a period of natural repose, it is not rendered abortive. Eventually every spiritual monad - itself a sinless unconscious principle, will work through conscious forms on lower levels, until these, throwing off one after another higher and higher forms, will produce that in which the God-like consciousness may be fully evoked. Certainly it is not by reason of the grandeur of any human conceptions as to what would be an adequate reason for the existence of the universe, that such a consummation can appear an insufficient purpose, not even if the final destiny of the planetary spirit himself, after periods to which his development from the mineral forms of primaeval worlds is but a childhood in the recollection of the man, is to merge his glorified individuality into that sum total of all consciousness, which esoteric metaphysics treat as absolute consciousness, which is non-consciousness. These paradoxical expressions are simply counters representing ideas that the human mind is not qualified to apprehend, and it is waste of time to haggle over them.

These considerations supply the key to esoteric Buddhism, a more direct outcome of the universal esoteric doctrine than any other popular religion, for the effort in its construction has been to make men love virtue for its own sake and for its good effect on their future incarnations, not to keep them in subjection to any priestly system or dogma by terrifying their fancy with the doctrine of a personal judge waiting to try them for more than their lives at their death. Mr Lillie is mistaken, admirable as his intention has been, and sympathetic as his mind evidently is with the beautiful morality and aspiration of Buddhism, in deducing from its Temple ritual the notion of a Personal God. No such conception enters into the great esoteric doctrine of Nature, of which this volume has furnished an imperfect sketch. Not even in reference to the farthest regions of the immensity beyond our own planetary system, does the adept exponent of the esoteric doctrine tolerate the adoption of an agnostic attitude. It will not suffice for him to say, "As far as the elevated senses of planetary spirits, whose cognition extends to the outermost limits of the starry heavens - as far as their vision can extend, Nature is self-sufficing; as to what may lie beyond, we offer no hypothesis." What the adept really says on this head is, "The universe is boundless, and it is a stultification of thought to talk of any hypothesis setting in beyond the boundless - on the other side of the limits of the limitless."

That which antedates every manifestation of the universe, and would lie beyond the limit of manifestation, if such limits could ever be found, is that which underlies the manifested universe within our own purview - matter animated by motion, its Parabrahm or Spirit. Matter, space, motion, and duration, constitute one and the same eternal substance of the universe. There is nothing else eternal absolutely. That is the first state of matter, itself perfectly uncognizable by physical senses, which deal with manifested matter, another state altogether. But though thus in one sense of the word materialistic, the esoteric doctrine, as any reader of the foregoing explanations will have seen, is as far from resembling the gross narrow-minded conception of Nature, which ordinary goes by the name of Materialism, as the North Pole looks away from the South. It stoops to Materialism, as it were, to link its methods with the logic of that system, and ascends to the highest realms of idealism, to embrace and expound the most exalted aspirations of Spirit. As it cannot be too frequently or earnestly repeated - it is the union of Science and Religion - the bridge by which the most acute and cautious pursuers of experimental knowledge may cross over to the most enthusiastic devotee, by means of which the most enthusiastic devotee may return to Earth and yet keep Heaven still around him.

# CHAPTER XII

## The Doctrine Reviewed

Long familiarity with the esoteric doctrine will alone give rise to a full perception of the manner in which it harmonizes with facts of Nature such as we are all in a position to observe. But something may be done to indicate the correspondences that may be traced between the whole body of teaching now set forth and the phenomena of the world around us.

Beginning with the two great perplexities of ordinary philosophy " the conflict between free-will and predestination, and the origin of evil, it will surely be recognized that the system of Nature now explained enables us to deal with those problems more boldly than they have ever yet been handled. Till now the most prudent thinkers have been least disposed to profess that either by the aid of metaphysics or religion could the mystery of free-will and predestination be unraveled. The tendency of thought has been to relegate the whole enigma to the region of the unknowable. And, strange to say, this has been done contentedly by people who have been none the less contented to accept as more than a provisional hypothesis the religious doctrines which thus remained incapable of reconciliation with some of their own most obvious consequences. The omniscience of a personal Creator, ranging over the future as well as the past, left man no room to exercise the independent authority over his own destinies which nevertheless it was absolutely necessary to allow him to exercise in order that the policy of punishing or rewarding him for his acts in life could be recognized as anything but the most grotesque injustice. One great English philosopher, frankly facing the embarrassment, declared in a famous posthumous essay that, by reason of these considerations, it was impossible that God could be all-good and all-potent. People were free to invest him logically with one or other of these attributes, but not with both. The argument was treated with the respect due to the great reputation of its author, and put aside with the discretion due to respect for orthodox tenets.

But the esoteric doctrine comes to our rescue in this emergency. First of all it honestly takes into account the insignificant size of this world compared to the universe. This is a fact of Nature which the early Christian church feared with a true instinct, and fought with the cruelty of terror. The truth was denied, and its authors were tortured for many centuries. Established at last beyond even the authority of papal negations, the Church resorted to the "desperate expedient," to quote Mr Rhys David's phrase, of pretending that it did not matter.

The pretense till now has been more successful than its authors could have hoped. When they dreaded astronomical discovery, they were crediting the world at large with more remorseless logic than it ultimately showed any inclination to employ. People have been found willing as a rule to do that which I have described esoteric Buddhism as not requiring us to do, to keep their science and their religion in separate water-tight compartments. So long and so thoroughly has this principle been worked upon, that it has finally ceased to be an argument against the credibility of a religious dogma to point out that it is impossible. But when we establish a connection between our hitherto divided reservoirs, and require them to stand at the same level, we cannot fail to see how the insignificance of the earth's magnitude diminishes in a corresponding proportion the plausibility of theories that require us to regard the details of our own lives as part of the general stock of a universal Creator's omniscience. On the contrary, it is unreasonable to suppose that the creatures inhabiting one of the smaller planets of one of the smaller suns in the ocean of the universe, where suns are but water-drops in the sea, are exempt in any way from the general principle of government by law. But that principle cannot co-exist with government by caprice, which is an essential condition of such predestination as conventional discussions of the problems before us associate with the use of the word. For be it observed that the predestination which conflicts with free-will is not the predestination of races, but individual predestination, associated with the ideas of divine grace of wrath. The pre-destination of races, under laws analogous to those which control the general tendency of any multitude of independent chances, is perfectly compatible with individual free-will, and thus it is that the esoteric doctrine reconciles the long-standing contradiction of Nature. Man has control over his own destiny within constitutional limits, so to speak; he is perfectly free to make use of his natural rights as far as they go, and they go practically to infinity as far as he, the individual unit, is concerned. But the average human action, under given conditions, taking a vast multiplicity of units into account, provides for the unfailing evolution of the cycles which constitute their collective destiny.

Individual predestination, it is true, may be asserted, not as a religious dogma having to do with divine grace or wrath, but on purely metaphysical grounds " that is to say, it may be argued that each human creature is fundamentally, in infancy, subject to the same influence by similar circumstances, and that an adult life is thus merely the product or impression of all the circumstances which have influenced such a life from the beginning, so that, if those circumstances were known, the moral and intellectual result would be known. By this train of reasoning it can be made to appear that the circumstances of each man's life may be theoretically knowable by a sufficiently searching intelligence; that hereditary tendencies, for example, are but products of antecedent circumstances entering into any given calculation as a perturbation, but not the less calculable on that account. This contention, however, is no less in direct conflict with the consciousness of humanity, than the religious dogma of individual predestination. The sense of free-will is a factor in the process which cannot be ignored, and the free-will of which we are thus sensible is not a mere automatic impulse, like the twitching of a dead frog's leg. The ordinary religious dogma and the ordinary metaphysical argument both require us to regard it in that light; but the esoteric doctrine restores it to its true dignity, and shows us the scope of its activity, the limits of its sovereignty. It is sovereign over the individual career, but impotent in presence of the cyclic law, which even so positive a philosopher as Draper detects in human history " brief as the period is which he is enabled to observe. And none the less does that collateral quicksand of thought which J S Mill discerned alongside the contradictions of theology " the great question whether speculation must work with the allgood or all-potent hypothesis " find its explanation in the system now disclosed. Those great beings, the perfected efflorescence of former humanity, who, though far from constituting a supreme God, reign nevertheless in a divine way over the destinies of our world, are not only not omnipotent, but, great as they are, are restricted as regards their action by comparatively narrow limits. It would seem as if, when the stage is, so to speak, prepared afresh for a new drama of life, they are able to introduce some improvements into the action, derived from their own experience in the drama with which they were concerned, but are only capable, as regards the main construction of the piece, of repeating that which has been represented before. They can do on a large scale what a gardener can do with dahlias on a small one; he can evolve considerable improvements in form and colour, but his flowers, however carefully tended, will be dahlias still.

Is it nothing, one may ask in passing, in support of the acceptability of the esoteric doctrine, that natural analogies support it at every turn? As it is below, so it is above, wrote the early occult philosophers; the microcosm is a mirror of the macrocosm. All Nature lying within the sphere of our physical observation verifies the rule, so far as that limited area can exhibit any principles. The structure of lower animals is reproduced with modifications in higher animals, and in Man; the fine fibres of the leaf ramify like the branches of the tree, and the microscope follows such ramifications, repeated beyond the range of the naked eye. The dust-laden currents of rain-water by the roadside deposit therein "sedimentary rocks" in the puddles they develop, just as the rivers do in the lakes and the great waters of the world over the sea-bed. The geological work of a pond and that of an ocean differ merely in their scale, and it is only in scale that the esoteric doctrine shows the sublimest laws of Nature differing in their jurisdiction over the man, and their jurisdiction over the planetary family. As the children of each human generation are tended in infancy by their parents, and grow up to tend another generation in their turn, so in the whole humanity of the great manvantaric periods, the men of one generation grow to be the Dhyan Chohans of the next, and then yield their places in the ultimate progress of time to their descendants, and pass themselves to higher conditions of existence.

Not less decisively than it answers the question about free-will, does the esoteric doctrine deal with the existence of evil. This subject has been discussed in its place in the preceding chapter on the Progress of Humanity; but the esoteric doctrine, it will be seen, grapples with the great problem more closely than by the mere enunciation of the way human free-will, which it is the purpose of Nature to grow and cultivate into Dhyan Chohanship, must by the hypothesis be free to develop evil itself, if it likes. So much for the broad principle in operation, but the way it works is traceable in the present teaching as clearly as the principle itself. It works through physical Karma, and could not but work that way, except by a suspension of the invariable law that causes cannot but produce effects. The objective man born into the physical world is just as much the creation of the person he last animated, as the subjective man who has in the interim been living the Devachanic existence. The evil that men do lives after them, in a more literal sense even than Shakespeare intended by those words. It may be asked, how can the moral guilt of a man in one life cause him to be born blind or crippled at a different period of the world's history several thousand years later, of parents with whom he has had, through his former life, no sort of physical connection whatever? But the difficulty is met, by considering the operation of affinities, more easily than may be imagined at the first glance. The blind or crippled child as regards his physical frame, may have been the potentiality rather than the product of local circumstances. But he would not have come into existence unless there had been a spiritual monad pressing forward for incarnation and bearing with it a fifth principle (so much of a fifth principle as is persistent, of course) precisely adapted by its Karma to inhabit that potential body. Given these circumstances, and the imperfectly organized child is conceived and brought into the world, to be a cause of trouble to himself and others " an effect becoming a cause in its turn " and a living enigma for philosophers endeavouring to explain the origin of evil.

The same explanation applies with modifications to a vast range of cases that might be cited to illustrate the problem of evil in the world. Incidentally, moreover, it covers a question connected with the operation of the Karmic law that can hardly be called a difficulty, as the answer would probably be suggested by the bearings of the doctrine itself, but is none the less entitled to notice. The selective assimilation of Karmaladen spirits with parentage which corresponds to their necessities or deserts, is the obvious explanation which reconciles rebirth with atavism and heredity. The child born may seem to reproduce the moral and mental peculiarities of parents or ancestors as well as their physical likeness, and the fact suggests the notion that his soul is as much an offshoot of the family tree as his physical frame. It is unnecessary to enlarge here on the multifarious embarrassments by which that theory would be surrounded, on the extravagance of supposing that a soul thus thrown off, like a spark from an anvil, without any spiritual past behind it, can have a spiritual future before it. The soul, which was thus merely a function of the body, would certainly come to an end with the dissolution of that out of which it arose. The esoteric doctrine, however, as regards transmitted characteristics, will afford a complete explanation of that phenomenon, as well as of all others connected with human life. The family into which he is born is, to the re-incarnating spirit, what a new planet is to the whole tide of humanity on a round along the manvantaric chain. It has been built up by a process of evolution working on a line transverse to that of humanity's approach; but it is fit for humanity to inhabit when the time comes. So with the re-incarnating spirit, it presses forward into the objective world, the influences which have retained it in the Devachanic state having been exhausted, and it touches the spring of Nature, so to speak, provoking the development of a child which without such an impulse would merely have been a potentiality, not an actual development; but in whose parentage it finds " of course unconsciously by the blind operation of its affinities " the exact conditions of renewed life for which it has prepared itself during its last existence. Certainly we must never forget the presence of exceptions in all broad rules of Nature. In the present case it may sometimes happen that mere accident causes an injury to a child at birth. Thus a crippled frame may come to be bestowed on a spirit whose Karma has by no means earned that penalty, and so with a great variety of accidents. But of these all that need be said is that Nature is not at all embarrassed by her accidents; she has ample time to repair them. The undeserved suffering of one life is amply redressed under the operation of the Karmic law in the next, or the next. There is plenty of time for making the account even, and the adepts declare, I believe, that, as a matter-of-fact, in the long-run undeserved suffering operates as good luck rather than otherwise, thereby deriving from a purely scientific observation of facts a doctrine which religion has benevolently invented sometimes for the consolation of the afflicted.

While the esoteric doctrine affords in this way an unexpected solution of the most perplexing phenomena of life, it does this at no sacrifice in any direction of the attributes we may fairly expect of a true religious science. Foremost among the claims we may make on such a system is that it shall contemplate no injustice, either in the direction of wrong done to the undeserving, or of benefits bestowed on the undeserving; and the justice of its operation must be discernible in great things and small alike. The legal maxim, *de minimis non curat lex*, is means of escape for human fallibility from the consequences of its own imperfections. There is no such thing as indifference to small things in chemistry or mechanics. Nature in physical operations responds with exactitude to small causes as certainly as to great, and we may feel instinctively sure that in her spiritual operations also she has no clumsy habit of treating trifles as of no consequence, of ignoring small debts in consideration of paying big ones, like a trader of doubtful integrity content to respect obligations which are serious enough to be enforced by law. Now the minor acts of life, good and bad alike, are of necessity ignored under any system which makes the final question at stake, admission to or exclusion from a uniform or approximately uniform condition of blessedness. Even as regards that merit and demerit which is solely concerned with spiritual consequences, no accurate response could be made by Nature except by means of that infinitely graduated condition of spiritual existence described by the esoteric doctrine as the Devachanic state. But the complexity to be dealt with is more serious than even the various conditions of Devachanic existence can meet. No system of consequences ensuing to mankind after the life now under observation, can be recognized as adapted scientifically to the emergency, unless it responds to the sense of justice, in regard to the multifarious acts and habits of life generally, including those which merely relate to physical existence, and are not deeply coloured by right or wrong.

Now, it is only by a return to physical existence that people can possibly be conceived to reap with precise accuracy the harvest of the minor causes they may have generated when last in objective life. Thus, on a careful examination of the matter, the Karmic law, so unattractive to Buddhist students, hitherto, in its exoteric shape, and no wonder, will be seen not only to reconcile itself to the sense of justice, but to constitute the only imaginable method of natural action that would do this. The continued individuality running through successive Karmic rebirths once realized, and the corresponding chain of spiritual existences intercalated between each, borne in mind, the exquisite symmetry of the whole system is in no way impaired by that feature which seems obnoxious to criticism at the first glance, " the successive baths of oblivion through which the reincarnating spirit has to pass. On the contrary, that oblivion itself is in truth the only condition on which objective life could fairly be started afresh. Few earthlives are entirely free from shadows, the recollection of which would darken a renewed lease of life for the former personality. And if it is alleged that the forgetfulness in each life, of the last, involves waste of experience and effort, and intellectual acquirements, painfully or laboriously obtained, that objection can only be raised in forgetfulness of the Devachanic life in which, far from being wasted, such efforts and acquirements are the seeds from which the whole magnificent harvest of spiritual results will be raised. In the same way the longer the esoteric doctrine occupies the mind, the more clearly it is seen that every objection brought against it meets with a ready reply, and only seems an objection from the point of view of imperfect knowledge.

Passing from abstract considerations to others partly interwoven with practical matters, we may compare the esoteric doctrine with the observable facts of Nature in several ways with the view of directly checking its teachings. A spiritual science which has successfully divined the absolute truth must accurately fit the facts of earth whenever it impinges on earth. A religious dogma in flagrant opposition to that which is manifestly truth in respect of geology and astronomy, may find churches and congregations content to nurse it, but is not worth serious philosophical consideration. How then does the esoteric doctrine square with geology and astronomy?

It is not too much to say that it constitutes the only religious system that blends itself easily with the physical truths discovered by modern research in those branches of science. It not only blends itself with, in the sense of tolerating, the nebula hypothesis and the stratification of rocks, it rushes into the arms of these facts, so to speak, and could not get on without them. It could not get on without the great discoveries of modern biology; and, as a system recommending itself to notice in a scientific age, it could ill afford to dispense with the latest acquisitions of physical geography.

The stratification of the earth's crust is, of course, a plain and visible record of the inter-racial cataclysms. Physical science is emerging from the habits of timidity which its insolent oppression by religious bigotry for fifteen centuries engendered, but it is still a little shy in its relations with dogma, from the mere force of habit. In that way geology has been content to say, such and continents, as their shell-beds testify, must have been more than once submerged below and elevated above the surface of the ocean. It has not yet grown used to the free application of its own materials to speculation which trenches upon religious territory. But surely if geology were required to interpret all its facts into a consistent history of the earth, throwing in the most plausible hypotheses it could invent to fill up gaps in its knowledge, it would already construct a history for mankind which in its broad outlines would not be unlike that sketched out in the foregoing chapter on the Great World Periods; and the further geological discovery progresses, our esoteric teachers assure us, the more closely will the correspondence of the doctrine and the bony traces of the past be recognized. Already we find experts from the Challenger vouching for the existence of Atlantis, though the subject belongs to a class of problems unattractive to the scientific world generally, so that the considerations in favour of the lost continent are not yet generally appreciated. Already thoughtful geologists are quite ready to recognize that in regard to the forces which have fashioned the earth, this, the period within the range of historic traces, may be a period of comparative inertia and slow change; that cataclysmal metamorphoses may have been added formerly to those of gradual subsidence, upheaval, and denudation. It is only a step or two to the recognition as a fact, of what no one could any longer find fault with as a hypothesis, that great continental upheavals and submergences take place alternately; that the whole map of the world is not only thrown occasionally into new shapes, like the pictures of a kaleidoscope as its coloured fragments fall into new arrangements, but subject to systematically recurrent changes, which restore former arrangements at enormous intervals of time.

Pending further discoveries, however, it will, perhaps, be admitted that we have a sufficient block of geological knowledge already in our possession to fortify the cosmogony of the esoteric doctrine. That the doctrine should have been withheld from the world generally as long as no such knowledge had paved the way for its reception can hardly be considered indiscreet for the part of its custodians. Whether the present generation will attach sufficient importance to its correspondence with what has been ascertained of Nature in other ways remains to be seen.

These correspondences may, of course, be traced in biology as decisively as in geology. The broad Darwinian theory of the Descent of Man from the animal kingdom is not the only support afforded by this branch of science to the esoteric doctrine. The detailed observations now carried out in embryology are especially interesting for the light they throw on more than one department of this doctrine. Thus the now familiar truth that the successive stages of ante-natal human development correspond to the progress of human evolution through different forms of animal life, is nothing less than a revelation, in its analogical bearings. It does not merely fortify the evolutionary hypothesis itself, it affords a remarkable illustration of the way Nature works in the evolution of new races of men at the beginning of the great round-periods. When a child has to be developed from a germ which is so simple in its constitution that it is typical less of the animal " less even of the vegetable " than of the mineral kingdom, the familiar scale of evolution is run over, so to speak, with a rapid touch. The ideas of progress which may have taken countless ages to work out in a connected chain for the first time, are once for all firmly lodged in Nature's memory, and thenceforth they can be quickly recalled in order in a few months. So with the new evolution of humanity on each planet as the human tide-wave of life advances. In the first round the process is exceedingly slow, and does not advance far. The ideas of Nature are themselves under evolution. But when the process has been accomplished once, it can be quickly repeated. In the later rounds the life-impulse runs up the gamut of evolution with a facility only conceivable by help of the illustration which embryology affords. This is the explanation of the way the character of each round differs from its predecessor. The evolutionary work which has been once accomplished is soon repeated; then the round performs its own evolution at a very different rate, as the child, once perfected up to the human type, performs its own individual growth but slowly, in proportion to the earlier stages of its initial development.

No elaborate comparison of exoteric Buddhism with the views of Nature, which have now been set forth " briefly indeed, considering their scope and importance, but comprehensively enough to furnish the reader with a general idea of the system in its whole enormous range " will be required from me. With the help of the information now communicated, more experienced students of Buddhist literature will be better able to apply to the enigmas that may contain, the keys which will unlock their meaning. The gaps in the public records of Buddha's teaching will be filled up readily enough now, and it will be plain why they were left. For example, in Mr Rhys Davids' book, I find this: "Buddhism does not attempt to solve the problem of the primary origin of all things;" and quoting from Hardy's *Manual of Buddhism,* he goes on, "When Malunka asked the Buddha whether the existence of the world is eternal or not eternal, he made him no reply; but the reason of this was that it was considered by the teacher as an inquiry that tended to no profit." In reality the subject was manifestly passed over because it could not be dealt with by a plain yes or no, without putting the inquirer upon a false scent; while to put him on the true scent would have required a complete exposition of the whole doctrine about the evolution of the planetary chain, an explanation of that for which the community Buddha was dealing with, was not intellectually ripe. To infer from his silence that he regarded the inquiry itself as tending to no profit, is a mistake which may naturally enough have been made in the absence of any collateral knowledge, but none can be more complete in reality. No religious system that ever publicly employed itself on the problem of the origin of all things, has, as will now be seen, done more than scratch the surface of that speculation, in comparison with the exhaustive researches of the esoteric science of which Buddha was no less prominent an exponent than he was a prominent teacher of morals for the populace.

The positive conclusions as to what Buddhism does teach " carefully as he has worked them out " are no less inaccurately set forth by Mr Rhys Davids than the negative conclusion just quoted. It was inevitable that all such conclusions should hitherto be inaccurate. I quote an example, not to disparage the careful study of which it is the fruit , but to show how the light now shed over the whole subject penetrates every cranny, and puts an entirely new complexion on all its features.

"Buddhism takes as its ultimate fact the existence of the material world, and of conscious beings, living within it; and it holds that everything is subject to the law of cause and effect, and that everything is constantly, though imperceptibly, changing. There is no place where this law does not operate; no heaven or hell therefore in the ordinary sense. There are worlds where angels live whose existence is more or less material according as their previous lives were more or less holy; but the angels die, and the worlds they inhabit pass away. There are places of torment where the evil actions of men or angels produce unhappy beings; but when the active power of the evil that produced them is exhausted, they will vanish, and the worlds they inhabit are not eternal. The whole Kosmos " earth and heavens, and hells " is always tending to renovation or destruction, is always in a course of change, a series of revolutions or of cycles, of which the beginning and the end alike are unknowable and unknown. To this universal law of composition and dissolution, men and gods form no exception; the unity of forces which constitutes a sentient being must sooner or later be dissolved, and it is only through ignorance and delusion that such a being indulges in the dream that it is a separable and self-existent entity."

Now, certainly this passage might be taken to show how the popular notions of Buddhist philosophy are manifestly thrown off from the real esoteric philosophy. Most assuredly that philosophy no more finds in the universe than in the belief of any truly enlightened thinker " Asiatic or European " the unchangeable and eternal heaven and hell of monkish legend; and "the worlds where angels live," and so on " the vividly real though subjective strata of the Devachanic state " *are* found in Nature truly enough. So with all the rest of the popular Buddhist conceptions just passed in review. But in their popular form they are the nearest caricatures of the corresponding items of esoteric knowledge. Thus the notion about individuality being a delusion, and the *ultimate* dissolution as such of the sentient being, is perfectly unintelligible without fuller explanations concerning the multitudinous aeons of individual life, in as yet, to us, inconceivable, but ever progressive, conditions of spiritual exaltation, which come before that unutterably remote mergence into the non-individualized condition. That condition certainly must be somewhere in futurity, but its nature is something which no uninitiated philosopher, at any rate, has ever yet comprehended by so much as the faintest glimmering guess. As with the idea of Nirvana, so with this about the delusion of individuality, writers on Buddhist doctrine derived from exoteric sources, have most unfortunately found themselves entangled with some of the remote elements of the great doctrine, under the impression that they were dealing with Buddhist views of conditions immediately succeeding this life, The statement, which is almost absurd, thus put out of its proper place in the whole doctrine, may be felt, not only as no longer an outrage on the understanding, but as a sublime truth, when restored to its proper place in relation to other truths. The ultimate mergence of the perfect Man-god or Dhyan Chohan in the absolute consciousness of paranirvana, has nothing to do, let me add, with the "heresy of individuality," which relates to physical personalities. To this subject I recur a little later on.

Justly enough, Mr Rhys Davids says, in reference to the epitome of Buddhist doctrine quoted above: "Such teachings are by no means peculiar to Buddhism, and similar ideas lie at the foundation of earlier Indian philosophies." (Certainly by reason of the fact that Buddhism, as concerned with doctrine, was earlier Indian philosophy itself.) "They are to be found indeed in other systems widely separated from them in time and place; and Buddhism, in dealing with the truth which they contain, might have given a more decisive and more lasting utterance, if it had not also borrowed a belief in the curious doctrine of transmigration, a doctrine which seems to have arisen independently, if not simultaneously, in the Valley of the Ganges and the Valley of the Nile. The word transmigration has been used, however, in different times and at different places for theories similar, indeed, but very different; and Buddhism, in adopting the general idea from post-Vedic Brahminism, so modified it as to originate, in fact, a new hypothesis. The new hypothesis, like the old one, related to life in past and future births, and contributed nothing to the removal here, in this life, of the evil it was supposed to explain."

The present volume should have dissipated the misapprehensions on which these remarks rest. Buddhism does not believe in anything resembling the passage backwards and forwards between animal and human forms, which most people conceive to be meant by the principle of transmigration. The transmigration of Buddhism is the transmigration of Darwinian evolution scientifically developed, or rather exhaustively explored, in both directions. Buddhist writings certainly contain allusions to former births, in which even the Buddha himself was now one and now another kind of animal. But these had reference to the remote course of pre-human evolution, of which his fully opened vision gave him a retrospect. Never in any authentic Buddhist writings will any support be found for the notion that any human creature, once having attained manhood, falls back into the animal kingdom. Again, while nothing indeed could be more ineffectual as an explanation of the origin of evil, than such a caricature of transmigration as would contemplate such a return, the progressive rebirths of human Egos into objective existence, coupled with the operation of physical Karma, and the inevitable play of free-will within the limits of its privilege, *do* explain the origin of evil, finally and completely. The effort of Nature being to grow a new harvest of Dhyan Chohans whenever a planetary system is evolved, the incidental development of transitory evil is an unavoidable consequence under the operation of the forces of processes just mentioned, themselves unavoidable stages in the stupendous enterprise set on foot.

At the same time the reader, who will now take up Mr Rhys Davids book and examine the long passage on this subject, and on the *skandhas*, will realize how utterly hopeless a task it was to attempt the deduction of any rational theory of the origin of evil from the exoteric materials there made use of. Nor was it possible for these materials to suggest the true explanation of the passage immediately afterwards quoted from the Brahmajala Sutra: "

"After showing how the unfounded belief in the eternal existence of God or gods arose, Gautama goes on to discuss the question of the soul, and points out thirty-two beliefs concerning it, which he declares to be wrong. These are shortly as follows: Upon what principle or on what ground, do these mendicants and Brahmans hold the doctrine of future existence? They teach that the soul is material, or is immaterial, or is both or neither; that it will have one or many modes of consciousness; that its perceptions will be few or boundless; that it will be in a state of joy or of misery or of neither. These are the sixteen heresies, teaching a conscious existence after death. Then there are eight heresies teaching that the soul material or immaterial, or both or neither, finite or infinite, or both or neither, has one unconscious existence after death. And, finally, eight others which teach that the soul, in the same eight ways, exists after death in a state of being neither conscious nor unconscious. Mendicants,' concludes the sermon, that which binds the teacher to existence (viz. *tanha*, thirst) is cut off, but his body still remains. While his body shall remain, he will be seen by gods and men, but after the termination of life, upon the dissolution of the body, neither gods nor men will see him.' Would it be possible in a more complete and categorical manner to deny that there is any soul " anything of any kind which continues to exist in any manner after death?"

Certainly, for exoteric students, such a passage as this could not but seem in flagrant contradiction with those teachings of Buddhism which deal with the successive passages of the same individuality through several incarnations, and which thus along another line of thought may seem to assume the existence of a transmissible soul, as plainly as the passage quoted denies it. Without a comprehension of the seven principles of man, no separate utterances on the various aspects of this question of immortality could possibly be reconciled. But the key now given leaves the apparent contradiction devoid of all embarrassment. In the passage last quoted Buddha is speaking of the astral personality, while the immortality recognized by the esoteric doctrine is that of the spiritual individuality. The explanation has been fully given in the chapter on Devachan, and in the passages quoted there from Colonel Olcott's *Buddhist Catechism*. It is only since fragments of the great revelation this volume contains have been given out during the last two years in The Theosophist [magazine] , that the important distinction between personality and individuality, as applied to the question of human immortality, has settled into an intelligible shape; but there are plentiful allusions in former occult writing, which may now be appealed to in proof of the fact that former writers were fully alive to the doctrine itself. Turning to the most recent of the occult books in which the veil of obscurity was still left to wrap the doctrine from careless observation, though it was strained in many places almost to transparency, we might take any one of a dozen passages to illustrate the point before us. Here is one:-

"The philosophers who explained the fall into generation their own way, viewed spirit as something wholly distinct from the soul. They allowed its presence in the astral capsule only so far as the spiritual emanations or rays of the "shining one" were concerned. Man and soul had to conquer their immortality by ascending toward the unity, with which, if successful, they were finally linked, and into which they were absorbed, so to say. The individualization of man after death depended on the spirit, not on his body and soul. Although the word personality' in the sense in which it is usually understood, is an absurdity if applied literally to our immortal essence, still the latter is a distinct entity, immortal and eternal *per se*, and as in the case of criminals beyond redemption, when the shining thread which links the spirit to the soul from the moment of the birth of a child, is violently snapped, and the disembodied entity is left to share the fate of the lower animals, to dissolve into ether, and have its individuality annihilated " even then the spirit remains a distinct being." [*Isis Unveiled,*" volume 1, Page 315]

No one can read this " scarcely any part, indeed, of the chapter from which it is taken " without perceiving, by the light of the explanations given in the present volume, that the esoteric doctrine, now fully given out, was perfectly familiar to the writer " though I have been privileged to put it for the first time into plain and unmistakable language.

It takes some mental effort to realize the difference between personality and individuality, but the craving for the continuity of personal existence " for the full recollection always of those transitory circumstances of our present physical life which make up the personality " is manifestly no more than a passing weakness of the flesh. For many people it will perhaps remain irrational to say that any person now living, with his recollections bounded by the years of his childhood, is the same individual as some one of quite a different nationality and epoch who lived thousands of years ago, or the same that will reappear after a similar lapse of time under some entirely new conditions in the future. But the feeling "I am I," is the same through the three lives, and through all the hundreds; for that feeling is more deeply seated than the feeling, "I am John Smith, so high, so heavy, with such and such property and relations." Is it inconceivable " as a notion in the mind " that John Smith, inheriting the gift of Tithonus, changing his name from time to time, marrying afresh every other generation or so, losing property here, coming into possession of property there, and getting interested as time went on in a great variety of different pursuits " is it inconceivable that such a person in a few thousand years should forget all circumstances connected with the present life of John Smith, just as if the incidents of that life for him had never taken place? And yet the Ego would be the same. If this is conceivable in the imagination, what can be inconceivable in the individual continuity of an *intermittent* life, interrupted and renewed at regular intervals, and varied with passages through a purer condition of existence.

No less than it clears up the apparent conflict between the identify of successive individualities and the "heresy" of individuality, will the esoteric doctrine be seen to put the "incomprehensible mystery" of Karma, which Mr Rhys Davids disposes of so summarily, on a perfectly intelligible and scientific basis. Of this he says that because Buddhism "does not acknowledge a soul," it has to resort to the desperate expedient of a mystery to bridge over the gulf between one life and another somewhere else, the doctrine, namely, of Karma. And he condemns the idea as a "non-existent fiction of the brain." Irritated as he feels with what he regards as the absurdity of the doctrine, he yet applies patience and great mental ingenuity in the effort to evolve something that shall feel like a rational metaphysical conception out of the tangled utterances concerning Karma of the Buddhist scriptures. He writes: "

"Karma, from a Buddhist point of view, avoids the superstitious extreme, on the one hand, of those who believe in the separate existence of some entity called the soul; and the irreligious extreme on the other of those who do not believe in moral justice and retribution. Buddhism claims to have looked through the word soul for the fact it purports to cover, and to have found no fact at all, but only one or other of twenty different delusions which blind the eyes of men. Nevertheless, Buddhism is convinced that if a man reaps sorrow, disappointment, pain, he himself and no other must at some time have sown folly, error, sin, and if not in this life, then in some former birth. Where, then, in the latter case, is the identity between him who sows and him who reaps? *In that which alone remains* when a man dies, and the constituent parts of the sentient being are dissolved, in the result, namely, of his action, speech, and thought, in his good or evil Karma (literally his doing), which *does not* die. We are familiar with the doctrine, 'Whatever a man soweth, that shall he also reap,' and can therefore enter into the Buddhist feeling that whatever a man reaps that he must also have sown; we are familiar with the doctrine of the indestructibility of force, and can therefore understand the Buddhist dogma (however it may contravene our Christian notions) that no exterior power can destroy the fruit of a man's deeds, that they must work out their full effect to the pleasant or the bitter end. But the peculiarity of Buddhism lies in this, that the result of what a man is or does is held not to be dissipated, as it were, into many separate streams, but to be concentrated together in the formation of one new sentient being " new, that is, in its constituent parts and powers, but the same in its essence, its being, its doing, its Karma."

Nothing could be more ingenious as an attempt to invent for Buddhism an explanation of its "mystery" on the assumption that the authors of the mystery threw it up originally as a "desperate expedient" to cover their retreat from an untenable position. But in reality the doctrine of Karma has a far simpler history, and does not need so subtle an interpretation. Like many other phenomena of Nature having to do with futurity, it was declared by Buddha an incomprehensible mystery, and questions concerning it were thus put aside, but he did not mean that because it was incomprehensible for the populace, it was incomprehensible or any mystery at all for the initiates in the esoteric doctrine. It was impossible to explain it without reference to the esoteric doctrine, but the outlines of that science once grasped, Karma, like so much else, becomes a comparatively simple matter, a mystery only in the sense in which also the affinity of sulphuric acid for copper, and its superior affinity for iron, are also mysteries. Certainly esoteric science for *its* "lay chelas" at all events, like chemical science for its lay chelas, " all students, that is to say, of its mere physical phenomena, " leaves some mysteries unfathomed in the background. I am not prepared to explain by what precise molecular changes the higher affinities which constitute Karma are stored up in the permanent elements of the fifth principle. But no more is ordinary science qualified to say what it is in a molecule of oxygen, which induces it to desert the molecule of hydrogen with which it was in alliance in the raindrop, and attach itself to a molecule of the iron of a railing on which it falls. But the speck of rust is engendered, and a scientific explanation of that occurrence is held to have been given when its affinities are ascertained and appealed to.

So with Karma, the fifth principle takes up the affinities of its good and evil deeds in its passage through life, passes with them into Devachan, where those which are suitable to the atmosphere, so to speak, of that state, fructify and blossom in prodigious abundance, and then passes on, with such as have not yet exhausted their energy, into the objective world once more. And as certainly as the molecule of oxygen brought into the presence of a hundred other molecules will fly to that with which it has the most affinity, so will the Karma-laden spiritual monad fly to that incarnation with which its mysterious attractions link it. Nor is there in that process any creation of a new sentient being, except in the sense that the new bodily structure evolved is a new instrument of sensation. That which inhabits it, that which feels joy or sorrow, is the old Ego " walled off by forgetfulness from its last set of adventures on earth, it is true, but reaping their fruit nevertheless " the same "I am I" as before.

"Strange it is," Mr Rhys Davids thinks, that "all this," the explanation of Buddhist philosophy which esoteric materials have enabled him to give, "should have seemed not unattractive, these 2300 years and more, to many despairing and earnest hearts " that they should have trusted themselves to the so seeming stately bridge which Buddhism has tried to build over the river of the mysteries and sorrows of life . . . . They have failed to see that the very keystone itself, the link between one life and another, is a mere word " this wonderful hypothesis, this airy nothing, this imaginary cause beyond the reach of reason " the individualized and individualizing grace of Karma."

It would have been strange indeed if Buddhism had been built on such a frail foundation; but its apparent frailty has been simply due to the fact that its mighty fabric of knowledge has hitherto been veiled from view. Now that the inner doctrine has been unveiled, it will be seen how little it depends for any item of its belief on shadowy subtleties of metaphysics. So far as these have clustered round Buddhism they have merely been constructed by external interpreters of stray doctrinal hints that could not be entirely left out of the simple system of morals prescribed for the populace.

In that which really constitutes Buddhism we find a sublime simplicity, like that of Nature herself " one law running into infinite ramifications " complexities of detail, it is true, as Nature herself is infinitely complex in her manifestations, however unchangeably uniform in her purposes, but always the immutable doctrine of causes and their effects, which in turn become causes again in an endless cyclic progression.

*finis*

# Bibliography

Blavatsky, H.P. *Isis Unveiled*, two Volumes, New York, 1877

Davids, Rhys, T. W. *Buddhism*, etc. New York, 1878

Draper, J. W. *History of the Intellectual Development of Europe*. New York, 1863

Flammarion, Camille. *La Resurrection et la Fin des Mondes*. Paris

Hardy, Robert Spence. *Manual of Buddhism, in its Modern Development*, translated from Singhalese mss. 2nd ed London, 1880

Levi,. Eliphas (pseudonym of Alphonse Louie Constant) *Dogme et Rituel de la Haute Magie*, Paris, 1861. (later translated by A. E. Waite as *Transcendental Magic*)

Lillie, Arthur. *Buddha and Early Buddhism*, Edinburgh, 1880

Olcott, Henry Steel. *Buddhist Catechism*, Madras, 1881

Oldenberg, Hermann. *Buddha: His Life, His Doctrine, His Order*, Translated by Hoey, London, 1882

*The Theosophist* (periodical) started by H.P. Blavatsky and issued continuously from Madras, India since 1879. Issues cited: October 1881; March 1882; June 1883.

Parchment Books is committed to publishing high quality Esoteric/Occult classic texts at a reasonable price.

With the premium on space in modern dwellings, we also strive - within the limits of good book design - to make our products as slender as possible, allowing more books to be fitted into a given bookshelf area.

Parchment Books is an imprint of Aziloth Books, which has established itself as a publisher boasting a diverse list of powerful, quality titles, including novels of flair and originality, and factual publications on controversial issues that have not found a home in the rather staid and politically-correct atmosphere of many publishing houses.

Titles Include:

| | |
|---|---|
| *The Signature of All Things* | Jacob Boehme |
| *Psychic Self-Defence* | Dion Fortune |
| *The Ancient Wisdom* | Annie Besant |
| *The Masters and the Path* | C W Leadbeater |
| *Man, His True Nature & Ministry* | Louis-Claude de St.-Martin |
| *Secret Doctrines of the Rosicrucians* | Magus Incognito |
| *Corpus Hermeticum* | (trans. GRS Mead) |
| *The Virgin of the World* | Hermes Trismegistus |
| *Raja Yoga* | Yogi Ramacharaka |
| *Theosophy* | Rudolf Steiner |
| *The Interior Castle* | St Teresa of Avila |
| *The Gospel of Thomas* | Anonymous |
| *Pistis Sophia* | (trans. GRS Mead) |
| *The Secret Destiny of America* | Manly P Hall |
| *Practical Mysticism* | Evelyn Underhill |
| *The Rosicrucian Mysteries* | Max Heindel |
| *The Conference of Birds* | Farid ud-Din Attar |
| *Meetings With Remarkable Men* | G I Gurdjieff |
| *The Everlasting Man* | G K Chesterton |
| *The Voice of the Silence* | H P Blavatsky |
| *War Is A Racket* | Maj.-General Smedley D. Butler |

Obtainable at all good online and local bookstores.

View Parchment Books' full list at: www.azilothbooks.com

We are a small, approachable company and would love to hear any of your comments and suggestions on our plans, products, or indeed on absolutely anything. Aziloth is also interested in hearing from aspiring authors whom we might publish. We look forward to meeting you. Contact us at:

info@azilothbooks.com.

## CATHEDRAL CLASSICS

Parchment Book's sister imprint, Cathedral Classics, hosts an array of classic literature, from ancient tomes to twentieth-century masterpieces, all of which deserve a place in your home. A small selection is detailed below:

| | |
|---|---|
| Mary Shelley | *Frankenstein* |
| H G Wells | *The Time Machine; The Invisible Man* |
| Niccolo Machiavelli | *The Prince* |
| Omar Khayyam | *The Rubaiyat of Omar Khayyam* |
| Joseph Conrad | *Heart of Darkness; The Secret Agent* |
| Jane Austen | *Persuasion; Northanger Abbey* |
| Oscar Wilde | *The Picture of Dorian Gray* |
| Voltaire | *Candide* |
| Bulwer Lytton | *The Coming Race* |
| Arthur Conan Doyle | *The Adventures of Sherlock Holmes* |
| John Buchan | *The Thirty-Nine Steps* |
| Friedrich Nietzsche | *Beyond Good and Evil* |
| George Eliot | *Silas Marner* |
| Henry James | *Washington Square* |
| Stephen Crane | *The Red Badge of Courage* |
| Ralph Waldo Emmerson | *Self-Reliance, and Other Essays, (series 1&2)* |
| Sun Tzu | *The Art of War* |
| Charles Dickens | *A Christmas Carol* |
| Fyodor Dostoyevsky | *The Gambler; The Double* |
| Virginia Wolf | *To the Lighthouse; Mrs Dalloway.* |
| Johann W Goethe | *The Sorrows of Young Werther* |
| Walt Whitman | *Leaves of Grass - 1855 edition* |
| Confucius | *Analects* |
| Anonymous | *Beowulf* |
| Anne Bronte | *Agnes Grey* |
| More | *Utopia* |
| Farid ud-Din Attar | *The Conference of Birds* |
| Jack London | *Call of the Wild* |
| Edwin A. Abbott | *Flatland* |

full list at: www.azilothbooks.com

Obtainable at all good online and local bookstores.

www.ingramcontent.com/pod-product-compliance
Lightning Source LLC
Chambersburg PA
CBHW071701040426
42446CB00011B/1855